THE SECRET IS OUT

What People are Saying

Jessie is a woman after God's own heart. She is diligent in her desire to be the godly woman, wife, mother, sister, friend, and neighbor God has designed her to be. Her sincere faith draws others to Jesus, and you just cannot help but want what Jessie has with the Lord. When she shares, it is with grace, insight, and wisdom because she has gone deep into God's Word. Jessie is humble; she has a genuine love for women and a deep desire to teach them how to fulfill their God-given purposes. Invite Jessie to share at your next event, and you will surely "taste and see that the Lord is good."

Sally Hall
Director Precept Network, Precept Ministries International

When I began the *Secret is Out* study, I expected an in-depth study of God's Word through the book of Colossians. What I found was the godly wisdom for daily living that I desperately needed. Although I have walked with Jesus for years and have stacks of Bible studies to prove it, I was in a difficult season. The lessons were a balm to my wounded heart. The Scripture, personal study, and application taught me to move forward and take the next step no matter the circumstance or my feelings. Sometimes all I can see are my shortcomings and mistakes. What I learned was that I do not need to be perfect just to be consistently seeking HIM. Through this study of Colossians, I was reminded to forgive myself, to forgive others, and to continue clinging tightly to Jesus with every step of my daily walk.

Melissa Griffin
Facilitator

The guidance God gave me to take part in *The Secret is Out* is one I will be forever grateful for. This five-week informational and Spirit-filled study will be a blessing to all who dedicate their time and attention to it. Being a wife, mother of two teenage daughters, and the owner of my own business, time is a precious commodity. *The Secret is Out* will guide you into a deeper knowledge and understanding of the Book of Colossians in such a way that you can relate to without dedicating hours to research. After completing this study, you will have the information and Truth needed to live your life knowing and being confident that our Savior, Jesus Christ, lives in us!

Debra L. Snyder
Participant of The Secret is Out

I have known Jessie for the last ten years. She has been my mentor, encourager, and a dear sister in Christ. Her love for Christ is richly displayed in the pages of *The Secret is Out*, with confidence and sincerity. I have clung to Colossians 1:27, "Christ in me, the hope of glory," for the last few years. Studying *The Secret is Out* reignited my passion to tell others, with joy and boldness, about this Secret, Jesus Christ! My faith was strengthened, and I have a burning desire to love others with the love of Christ. Ladies, indulge yourself in this study so you can have "your mind set on things above." Share *The Secret is Out* with a girlfriend, and watch the love of Christ dwell richly in whom you share Jesus.

Jane Consiglio
Facilitator

The Secret is Out

Learn it. Live it. Pass it on.

Christ in You
A Study in Colossians

Jessie Seneca

THE SECRET IS OUT
Copyright © 2012 Jessie Seneca

ISBN 978-1-886068-54-4
Library of Congress Control Number: 2011946209
Published by Fruitbearer Publishing, LLC
P.O. Box 777, Georgetown, DE 19947
302.856.6649 • FAX 302.856.7742
www.fruitbearer.com • info@fruitbearer.com

Edited by Fran D. Lowe
Graphic design by Candy Abbott

Printed in the United States of America

Dedication

❦

To my loving husband, John.

Thank you for your support and encouragement that helped make this study possible. Your commitment to my dream made it reality.

Meet the Author

Jessie Seneca felt God calling her into a speaking/teaching ministry for women in 1996 when she attended a "Women of Faith" event. Having battled Cushing's syndrome, a life-threatening disease, she knew there was more to life than "just" surviving and that God was going to use her story in a way that would encourage women. At the time of her illness, it was hard for her to understand God's will in it all. Even when she felt God's call, she didn't know what it was going to look like. Through years of preparation and many encouraging individuals, today she is enjoying the fruit of her obedience to God through full-time ministry. Jessie feels that her life experiences equip her in a significant way to encourage women in their own personal walk with the Lord.

Jessie is the founder of *More of Him Ministries*, an organization grounded in the Word of God, providing her the opportunity to share with women in the U.S. and Canada. She enjoys seeing the difference the Word of God makes in the lives of women who immerse themselves in it. Her ministry challenges women to make God a priority and inspires them to move into a whole-hearted lifestyle, fully devoted to God. In addition to leading Bible studies, she enjoys conducting leadership training seminars.

God uses Jessie's passion and wisdom to speak into the lives of her listeners, and now, readers. *The Secret Is Out* is her first written Bible study, which grew out of a desire God placed in her heart to encourage women to have Jesus increase in their lives as they decrease (John 3:30, "He must become greater; I must become less").

Jessie lives in Pennsylvania with her husband, John, and her two daughters, Lauren and Sarah. You can find Jessie on many days walking her two dogs, Bella and Murphy.

Table of Contents

Facilitator's Guide

Welcome to *The Secret Is Out*. I am so glad you have decided to offer this study. My prayer is that you will be doubly blessed as you prepare for the women's group you facilitate.

Step One: Publicly promote *The Secret is Out* four to five weeks prior to the Introductory session.

Step Two: Order workbooks and DVDs.

Step Three: Reserve meeting rooms and DVD player.

Step Four: Enlist and meet with facilitators, if needed.

Leading a Discussion Group

You do not need to be a gifted teacher or natural leader to facilitate the small-group sessions. You should, however, have a desire to help women experience God's truth and the life-changing effect it can have on their lives. By your warm and hospitable demeanor,

you can encourage them to spend time with the Lord daily and enjoy His presence.

Before each session, view the DVD. Then, prayerfully and thoroughly prepare each week's assignment before meeting with your small group.

This guide will help facilitate six two-hour group sessions. Each DVD is suggested to be shown prior to the discussion time. The discussion should be less than an hour, with the remainder of your time devoted to prayer and fellowship.

During the Introductory Session

As women arrive, prepare name tags and tell them to pick up their copy of *The Secret Is Out*.

Welcome them and view the Introduction session together. A note page is provided for taking notes during the lecture.

After the introductory session, break up into small discussion groups of ten to twelve women and ask the women to introduce themselves to each other.

The facilitator should share with the women these "Four C" guidelines:

COMMITTED: We will get so much out of this study if we come prepared for the discussion and have spent time in His Word daily. May we be open to what God wants to show us in our lives (Psalm 139:23-24).

CONSIDERATE: We need to show consideration to the others in the group and be willing to serve them. We should be careful not to let anything we share bring harm to anyone's reputation. We also must not discuss the church or denomination we belong to, since many different churches are represented. We will also need to be courteous, letting others share, so that one or two people do not dominate the conversation. Each one of us needs to be sensitive to what God will have us share (Ephesians 5:21).

CONFIDENTIAL: Let this be a place where we can feel comfortable sharing. Let's give each other the assurance that no matter what we hear, we will respect another's feelings. No one should worry about being the focus of criticism or gossip (Ephesians 4:29).

CHRIST-LIKE: As we grow to know God more intimately, He will give us hope. He will change us and set us free to be all that He meant for us to be (2 Corinthians 3:18).

Suggestion: Ask the following questions pertaining to the introductory session:

- What excites you about the Book of Colossians?

- Have you encountered false teachings? If so, how did you handle them?

- How has God's Word changed your life?

- Do you find God's Word sweet? Why or why not?

- Is there an area in your life where you need to give Jesus first place?

- How does your life demonstrate that Jesus is your ALL in ALL?

End the discussion time with prayer. Encourage the women to prepare for Week One's discussion by completing their daily assignments from Week One.

During Sessions Two through Five

Welcome the women and view the session pertaining to the week together. The note page provided for taking notes during the lecture will accompany the assignment they completed during the week.

After the DVD session, break up into small discussion groups. You will find discussion questions marked by this symbol on each day:

These questions are formatted for the facilitator to conduct a discussion in a timely manner. You may ask additional questions as you feel led by the Holy Spirit.

End the discussion time with prayer. Encourage the women to prepare for the next week's discussion by completing their daily assignments.

During the Last Session Together

If you have a large group with multiple discussion groups, after viewing the DVD and before breaking up into your smaller discussion groups, you may want to have a corporate sharing time. During this discussion period, attendees will have the opportunity to share what God has taught them through *The Secret Is Out*. This is usually an emotionally moving and encouraging time for all participants.

I would love to hear from you about the impact this study has made on you and the women you lead through *The Secret Is Out*.

e-mail: jessie@jessieseneca.com

More of Him Ministries

Introduction

Welcome to this Bible study called *The Secret Is Out!* I am so thrilled that you have joined me for an in-depth look at the Book of Colossians. As we take this journey together, I hope you come to know this short but powerful letter inside and out. I pray that you will 1) *Learn It* for yourself, 2) *Live It Out* in a way that others notice the difference Christ has made in your life, and 3) desire to *Pass It On* to those you know.

After Jesus' death and resurrection, His apostles continued to spread the gospel throughout the world, but they encountered strong opposition by adherents of Judaism, pagan religion, Greek and Eastern religions, and mysticism. The world would not accept the simplicity of the gospel—that Jesus is the only way to God. So, the early church battled teachings that wanted to change or add to the pure and true gospel message. Because of Paul's heart for the believers of a church he may never have met in Colossae, about 120 miles inland from Ephesus, he encouraged them from a prison cell. Although the young Colossian church was growing in the Lord, Paul felt a need to warn them about the dangers of the teachings insisting that Christ alone is not enough. The apostle reminded the Colossians that because of Christ's supremacy and sufficiency, their completeness was in Him alone.

When I began to write this study, I must admit that I knew God had called me to dig into the Book of Colossians, but I didn't know what would come out of it. There are many "treasures" tucked into these four chapters. One of the greatest findings for me was that God has a secret. I thought, *What could that secret be?* This secret, "Christ in you, the hope of glory" (1:27), will unfold as you unpack the Scriptures for yourself. I pray that through *The Secret is Out* you will be grounded in the truth of Christ, the person of Christ, and the power of Christ. Finally, you will be challenged in your everyday relationships: the home, workplace, and church.

I primarily use the *New International Version* of the Bible in *The Secret is Out*. If you don't own one, you will still be able to answer the questions without difficulty. You will find discussion questions identified with a symbol like this:

HOW TO USE THIS STUDY: These questions are formatted for group study, ideally with your facilitator conducting discussion in a timely manner. But it will also be an effective tool if you want to undertake this study on your own. Either way, at the end of each day, I encourage you to take a moment to reflect on your day's findings and consider how God wants you to respond to what He showed you.

Through this study, God has taught me much about Himself and the continued renewal of mind, spirit, and soul that we need to seek out on a daily basis. I pray that whatever you do in word or deed, you do it all in the name of the Lord Jesus, giving thanks through Him to God the Father (3:17).

What I hope to gain from this study

Introductory Video Session

Colossians
Week One

Day One
Holy, Faithful, and True

Day Two
Our Eternal Cry Is—More

Day Three
The Visible Image

Day Four
The Secret Is Out

Day Five
Ministry Is Hard Work

Day One
Holy, Faithful, and True

I am so excited that you have joined me on this Colossians journey to seek, understand, and desire the greatest secret of all, which is *Christ in you*, the hope of glory.

My prayer is that we will grow in knowledge and understanding through studying together and that we will be grounded in the truth and power of Jesus Christ. I am up for the challenge. Are you? I would like you to know that there is a little more work in the first week of lesson material to lay the ground work. I hope you find it beneficial and challenging.

> The fear of the LORD is the beginning of knowledge.
> but fools despise wisdom and discipline.
> (Proverbs 1:7)

Let's begin by reading Colossians 1:1-2.

Paul's introduction to the Colossians:

1. Greeting by Paul (1:1-2).

2. Note of thanksgiving (1:3-8).

3. Prayer for spiritual wisdom (1:9-14).

Paul was not one of the original twelve disciples.

- Paul was an apostle. "Apostle" means "one sent out to preach the gospel."

- Paul was chosen by the will of God. Read Acts 9:1-19 to refresh your memory of Saul's (Paul's) conversion. In verse 15, what does it tell us about Paul?

_____

_____

_____

_____

Read the following Scriptures: Ephesians 1:4-5, 1 Peter 1:2, and Romans 8:29-30. **What do they reveal about God's chosen people?**

_____

_____

_____

_____

In Ephesians 1:4-5 and Romans 8:29, what does it say we are chosen for and predestined to become?

_____

_____

In 1 Peter 1:2, who works to bring about our salvation?

_____

_____

_____

This verse mentions all three members of the Trinity: God the Father, God the Son, and God the Holy Spirit.

List each one's role.

God the Father _____

God the Son _____

God the Holy Spirit _____

God = Chooses
Jesus Christ = Cleanses
Holy Spirit = Renews

GOD
CHOOSES

JESUS CHRIST
CLEANSES

HOLY SPIRIT
RENEWS

Can you recall your conversion?

Yours may not be as dramatic as Paul's, but it is still your story (testimony). God will use your personal testimony when you share it with others. Write down as many details as you can remember.

_____

_____

_____

_____

On the road to Damascus, Paul encountered Jesus and was changed forever (Acts 9:3-19). Paul became the "Champion of Faith." His life became transformed for the glory of God. Paul, once the persecutor of the church, became the preacher of the church.

Now let's consider Timothy. We will often find Timothy accompanying Paul. Paul picked up Timothy on his second missionary journey at Lystra, "where the brothers spoke well of him" (Acts 16:2).

- Timothy was like a son to Paul.

- First and 2 Timothy were written by Paul, as a leader, to Timothy and all believers to give him and us encouragement and instruction.

Dear sister, it is vital for our Christian walk to have others pouring into our lives and us pouring into others.

As I write this, I think of my dear friend, Dora, who is ninety-five years of age. Some of my most precious moments include sitting at her kitchen table, sharing her life, and learning from her example. I could name many others, but it would take up too much time, and I would forget someone. And yet, I think the most rewarding times for me have been pouring into others, on the opposite side of that table.

Are there women you can name who have poured into or influenced your life?

Name   What have they poured into you?

_____

_____

_____

_____

_____

Take a moment and pray for them, thanking God for their influence on your life. Let's make it our goal to emulate their "pouring" and bless others by exhibiting that same influence.

I am sure you can also think of some women who have not been a godly influence in your life. *(I wouldn't dare ask you to write their names, but recall them now in your mind.)*

Yes, we can learn from them as well—about what not to be and how not to act. I know for myself that my interactions with difficult people have provided some of the best learning experiences and teachable moments in my life.

Take a moment and thank God for them, including what you have learned from them.

_____

_____

_____

_____

_____

There are three reasons Paul felt it necessary to write to the Colossians:

1. To show the deity and supremacy of Christ in the face of the Colossian heresy,
2. To lead believers into spiritual maturity, and
3. To inform them of the state of affairs and elicit their prayers on Paul's behalf.[1]

In Colossians 1:2, who was Paul's letter written to?

_____

First, Paul is calling the Colossians *holy.*
- They were set apart by and for God.

Second, the Colossians are called *faithful.*
- They had a steadfast commitment to the gospel.

Third, they are referred to as ***brothers.***
- They are a family united in spirit, despite their differences in background and race.

HOLINESS IS
NOT A FEELING,
BUT THE END
PRODUCT OF
OBEDIENCE.

—Francis J. Roberts
*Come Away My
Beloved*

In the timeless devotional, *Come Away My Beloved,* Francis J. Roberts says, "Holiness is not a feeling, but the end product of obedience."

God used this special group of people in the Colossian church to make a difference. So, dear ones, not only is this letter for the Colossians, but for all believers set apart by God as well.

I know we are only looking at the first two verses of chapter 1 today, but there are such treasures to discover.

What two blessings do you see in Colossians 1:2 that are a gift from God?

_____

_____

Define grace and peace in your own words.

_____

_____

Grace – God's free and unmerited favor toward sinful man
Peace – freedom from discord; harmony in personal relationships, especially with God[2]

Please finish today's reading in **John 14:25-27** and **Philippians 4:6-7**. What gift did Jesus leave with us (John 14:27)?

_____

Deep and lasting peace is the end result of the Holy Spirit's work in our lives. It is God's permanent presence in our lives that guides and directs our paths.

Dear ones, we do not need to fear the present or future. If your life is full of stress or anxiety like so many women experience today, allow the Holy Spirit to fill you up with Christ's peace. Turn your worries into prayers. Whenever you start to worry, start to pray!

 What does Jesus' peace guard (Philippians 4:6-7)?

_____

God's peace will guard our emotions that flow from our hearts, as well as our perceptions that build up in our minds.

We must continue to pray for each other—that by the end of our weeks together, we will be more holy and faithful and have more sisterly love for each other. As we study, we will become more deeply grounded in God's Word, so we will enjoy the grace and peace that only comes from Him.

Reflective prayer:
Write your thoughts, convictions, or insights.

_____

_____

_____

_____

[1] John Walvoord and Roy Zuck, The Bible Knowledge Commentary, New Testament (Colorado Springs: Cook Communications), 668.

[2] Life Application Study Bible, New Living Translation (Wheaton, Illinois, Tyndale House Publishers, 1996).

Day Two
Our Eternal Cry is—More

Even though the Colossians were encountering false teachers at this time, Paul doesn't immediately address the false teachers. Instead, he shares with the Colossians the truth about the gospel and how it will positively affect their lives.

 Read Colossians 1:3-5 and list the three traits of Christian character/virtue that are evident in the lives of the Colossians.

1. _____

2. _____

3. _____

Colossians 1:6 tells us that the gospel message bears fruit in believers. The New Living Translation (NLT) says that it is changing lives everywhere.

**LOVE IS NOT A
FEELING; IT IS
BOTH AN
ATTITUDE AND
AN ACTION.**

Do others notice the trilogy of virtue in your life? Share with your group the recent evidence of God's power in your life.

Max Anders, editor of The Holman New Testament Commentary, says, "Faith is not a blind jump into the dark, but faith is being persuaded or convinced that something is true and trusting it with your life."[1] This faith involves trusting Jesus Christ.

Faith begins the process, but it is only the beginning.

> **Faith** looks upward to God.
> **Love** looks outward to others.
> **Hope** looks forward to the future.

Love is not a feeling; it is both an attitude and an action.

These three—*faith, love, and hope*—appear together throughout Paul's letters.

GO DEEPER

Look up the following Scriptures and identify the main points in each verse.

Galatians 5:5-6

_____

_____

_____

_____

_____

Hebrews 6:10-12; 10:22-24

_____

_____

_____

_____

_____

1 Peter 1:3-8, 21-22

_____

_____

_____

_____

_____

> We continually remember before our God and Father your work produced by faith, your labor prompted by love, and your endurance inspired by hope in our Lord Jesus Christ.
>
> (1 Thessalonians 1:3)

ADDITIONAL
NOTES

> But since we belong to the day, let us be self-controlled, putting on faith and love as a breastplate, and the hope of salvation as a helmet.
>
> (1 Thessalonians 5:8)

These virtues work together to make us active, hard-working believers able to endure the struggles of living in a fallen world. So, dear sister, continue to fill your days with the light and love of God! Continue to put your faith into action as the Colossians did so that your good work will be visible to those around you.

I once read, "You will know when you are listening to God when what you read in the Bible is what others see in your life." OUCH!

Read **Colossians 1:5.**

> The faith and love that spring from the hope that is stored up for you in heaven and that you have already heard about in the word of truth, the gospel.

What does this Scripture say our faith and love spring from?

_____

When we have the hope of eternal bliss, then out of that hope will spring faith and love.

Dear sister, how often do you think about the hope of heaven?

____ Occasionally   ____ Frequently   ____ Always   ____ Never

Christian hope is as certain, if not more certain, as tomorrow's dawn. It is the assurance that no matter how much we enjoy God's presence and blessings here on this earth, we will experience something far greater in heaven.

Write 1 Corinthians 2:9 and share what this means to you.

_____

_____

_____

_____

_____

Read Revelation 21:10-27 for a description of heaven (it will be worth the read).

Make some notes about God's heavenly home for His people.

_____

_____

_____

Now, if we have the hope of this eternal promise and the presence of the glory of God permanently, how can we live without this faith that produces love for others and the hope of a secure future?

Ladies, there is so much more than what this world has to offer. We are only passing through on a journey destined for our real home . . . HEAVEN.

Prayer: *May our faith draw love from You, O God, and our love express that faith to others.*

The apostle Paul was not only a good preacher; he also was a great pray-er. Many times when writing his letters, he would pause to break into prayer. Colossians 1:9-14 is one of those occasions.

Read Colossians 1:9-14. What is Paul's primary prayer request for his people?

_____

_____

_____

Paul's prayer was that God's people live a life worthy of the Lord, which includes pleasing Him. If you notice, Paul reminds us to pray for those who are doing well in the faith since they are the prime target for enemy attacks. He also wants us to include prayers for their spiritual growth and long-term development.

> Opposition is not only an evidence that God is blessing, but it is also an opportunity for us to grow. "God had one Son without sin," said Charles Spurgeon, "but He never had a son without a trial."
>
> —Warren Wiersbe

Read Nehemiah 4:11 to see why there are enemy attacks and conspiracies that creep into our good work. What does the Enemy want to accomplish?

Look back at Colossians 1:9. What does Paul ask God to do?

In the Greek, "fill" *(pleroma)* means (1) to be completely filled or (2) under the control of.[2] (3) A mere knowledge of God's Word is not what will please Him. Instead, we need to be controlled by that knowledge. Being controlled by God's will should cause us to do things we might not otherwise do, such as enduring rather than giving up and being patient with others rather than getting angry with them.[3]

Take a moment and identify an area in your life that you need God to take control of and ask for His infilling today.

Rabindranath Tagore, the Indian poet, once said, "The eternal cry is—more." Whatever the Colossians knew about God, there was so much more to discover and more infilling that needed to take place.

Discover truths about desiring God's infilling from the Book of Psalms. Look up and write what each verse means to you.

Psalm 42:1-2

ADDITIONAL NOTES

Psalm 63:1

_____

Psalm 143:6

_____

Isn't this awesome how we are growing in wisdom and understanding? As we continue to look at Paul's prayer in Colossians 1:10, we learn that our goal is to live a life worthy of the Lord and please Him in every way.

 If pleasing God is our goal, how do we achieve it? Paul spells it out very clearly in Colossians 1:10-12. Read it, and then write down the four areas that please God.

1. _____

2. _____

3. _____

4. _____

Continue to add to this list by writing Micah 6:8. Memorize this verse.

_____

_____

_____

_____

AND WITHOUT FAITH IT IS IMPOSSIBLE TO PLEASE GOD, BECAUSE ANYONE WHO COMES TO HIM MUST BELIEVE THAT HE EXISTS AND THAT HE REWARDS THOSE WHO EARNESTLY SEEK HIM.

—HEBREWS 11:6

Which of these areas is the most difficult for you at this season of your life and why?

_____

_____

_____

Dear sister, I ask myself so many times, Why can't I do this? How many times do I need to hear the Scripture before I apply it? We all go through periods of discouragement and wonder. I remember once sharing something with someone that I shouldn't have (Okay, gossip, you caught me). When I got in the car, I beat myself up over it. I could have stayed in that pit, but I heard God ask me in my spirit, *When was the last time you did that?* God was trying to show me how far I had come—that it had been longer between times of gossip than it used to be. I was encouraged to see that His power was at work in me, even though His work in me has not been completed yet. Praise the Lord! We need to keep pressing on. We need to keep striving to please God.

According to 2 Peter 1:3, whose power is it that helps us to please God?

_____

As we conclude today, finish by reading the end of Paul's prayer (Colossians 1:13-14).

What has God rescued us from?

_____

Where has He brought us?

_____

What do we have?

_____

To _redeem_ someone means "to buy them back and set them free." Jesus' death was the price paid to buy us back and set us free from both the penalty and the power of sin, bringing us out from the realm of darkness and placing us in the bright light of Jesus' kingdom. The Christian faith begins at the point of redemption.

Forgiveness parallels redemption. Forgive literally means "to send away; to cancel." Through the death of Jesus Christ, God has cancelled the debt of our sin.[4] We are considered a person without a past history. Amen, sister!

The question to you and me is this: Do we live as though we are forgiven, or do we still live caught in the snares of guilt?

Let's close with these comforting words from 1 John 1:9: "If we confess our sins, he is faithful and just and will forgive us our sins and purify us from all unrighteousness."

Today is a new day. Live life in the light of God's love for you!

**DO WE LIVE
AS THOUGH
WE ARE
FORGIVEN?**

Reflective prayer:

Write your thoughts, convictions, or insights.

_____

_____

_____

_____

_____

_____

_____

[1] Anders, Holman New Testament Commentary, 278.

[2] James Strong, The New Strong's Exhaustive Concordance of the Bible (Nashville: Thomas Nelson Publishers, 1990), 58.

[3] Anders, Holman New Testament Commentary, 281.

[4] Ibid., 282.

Day Three
The Visible Image

Before moving on to the doctrine of the supremacy of Christ, I want us to take a moment to revisit the phrase "walking worthy of the Lord" from yesterday's passage—Colossians 1:9-10. Paul prayed that "we would be filled with wisdom and understanding in order that we would live worthy of the Lord and please him in every way."

To the best of your knowledge, write what you believe "walking worthy of the Lord" means to you.

_____

_____

_____

_____

In the Greek, worthy *(axios)* means "of equal weight."[1] We are supposed to equal the Lord's standards—to be holy as He is holy.

ADDITIONAL
NOTES

Paul's aim in this petition was practical. A genuine knowledge of Christ reveals a transformed character in Christlikeness. Are you like me, sitting there in your chair, wondering, *How can I lead this lifestyle successfully?* Well, walking worthy of the Lord is a step-by-step process, one that begins by just focusing on the next step. Sometimes we become discouraged in the process because seeking victory seems overwhelming. If we are ever going to be the people God wants us to be, our focus needs only to be on the next step—and nothing else. We must walk moment by moment, hour by hour, and then day by day.

If you are trying to walk worthy of the Lord you may feel success is illusive. You probably find yourself good for a few days but then trip up. Remember, you are in the process of perfecting your walk. You are no different from anyone else. We all need the same power that comes from Christ (hint—yesterday we looked at 2 Peter 1:3) to walk worthy of the Lord. It is His divine power that enables us!

GO DEEPER

Look up the following Scriptures. Then record what it says about holiness and what we should strive for in our character.

Romans 13:12-14

_____

_____

_____

_____

Galatians 5:16-26

_____

_____

_____

_____

Ephesians 2:10

_____

_____

_____

_____

1 Peter 1:15-16

_____

_____

_____

_____

After reading these Scriptures, if you feel that you have a long way to go, just take your first step and strive for a life of worthiness. Continue to seek the Lord and draw from His power, not your own. Today is a new day!

I want to encourage you with the ending of Galatians 5:21: "Those who live like this will not inherit the kingdom of God." This does not say that Christians will lose their salvation if they lapse into a sin of the flesh. However, those who habitually indulge in these fleshly desires offer evidence that they may not be children of God.

Dear sister, there is hope. Yes, we have victory over these desires of the evil nature through Jesus Christ. If we are living in a vital union with Jesus Christ, we will have the Holy Spirit working through us (Acts 1:8) to display the fruit of the Spirit. In an ultimate sense this "fruit" is the personality of Christ lived out in a Christian.

 Write Galatians 5:22-23. These fruit are the by-products of Christ's control in our lives.

_____

_____

_____

Now we are going to move on to the main emphases of Colossians: the exaltation and preeminence of Christ. When Paul wrote to the Colossians, he was encountering false teachers everywhere. Even though they weren't encouraging the Colossians to forget about Jesus altogether, they basically were saying that He wasn't the "only show in town." They didn't negate the fact that Jesus could be prominent, but to them He certainly wasn't preeminent (first place).

GO DEEPER

 Read Colossians 1:13-18, Hebrews 1:1-4, Philippians 2:9-11, and 1 Corinthians 15:47 _(don't miss this one)._

Write an important characteristic you learned about Christ from these passages.

_____

_____

_____

_____

_____

_____

Wow! Christ is the visible image of the invisible God. In the Greek, image *(eikon)* means the essential embodiment of something or someone.[2] The word for image was used in Paul's time for a likeness placed on a coin and portraits, as well as sculpted into statues. It is closely related to our modern-day word "photograph."[3]

So, from these Scriptures, who do they say Jesus is the photograph of?

_____ A prophet   _____ A good teacher   _____ God

Is Jesus preeminent in your life? If not, what is hindering you from making and keeping Him first place in your life?

_____

I don't know about you, but I so love looking at the names of God. As I sat here reading this portion of Colossians, it reminded me of *El-Elyon,* which in the Hebrew means "Highest" or "Exalted One." When we praise the Most High, we are worshiping the One whose power, mercy, and sovereignty cannot be matched.

It took Nebuchadnezzar seven periods of time to figure it out, but in the end, he got it.

Read Daniel 4:24-26, 32, 34-35. What did Nebuchadnezzar come to understand?

With that single realization, light flooded Nebuchadnezzar's mind and his sanity returned. He reclaimed his throne with greater honor than before.

Dear sister, so it is with us. The unshakable fact of God's sovereign control over all is the foundation of our sanity in this crazed world. Do you trust Him with your life? He hems you in behind and before and places His hand of blessing on your head (Psalm 139:5).

These words clinch everything Paul said in Colossians 1:17: "In him all things hold together." One commentator said the opposite is, "Out of Him all things fly apart—they go to pieces." He went on to say that "everything in Him (Jesus) is centripetal; everything outside of Him is centrifugal."[4]

Do you ever feel like "life" is just out of control? Do you ever stop to wonder why? Does it have anything to do with you? I have felt this way many different times in my life, mainly because I just plainly wanted to control my life. Then I realized the problem with that statement: it was my life. I felt like I should be the one controlling it. After all, it's my life, right? It wasn't until I relinquished that control to God and let Him be the center of my life that peace began to take over.

Yesterday we looked at ways we can please God, but **what does Colossians 1:19 say about God's pleasure?**

What do you think this statement means: **"All his fullness dwells in Christ"?** (Also see Colossians 2:9.)

_____

_____

_____

Read John 14:23.

> Jesus replied, "If anyone loves me,
> he will obey my teaching.
> My Father will love him,
> and we will come to him
> and make our home with him."

If we love and obey Jesus,

    Who will love us?

    _____

    Who will come to us?

    _____

    And what will they do?

    _____

I can't get over that one little word "pleased." Did you notice that word as you read Colossians 1:19 and 2:9? The one person God dwells in without any pain is Jesus. Yes, He lives in us when we ask Him into our hearts, but it's not without some pain as He abides in us. One commentator put it like this: "God is at home in Jesus."[5]

ADDITIONAL NOTES

CHARACTER IS ALWAYS A CHOICE. DEVELOP YOUR CHARACTER ON THE INSIDE; THEN IT WILL FLOW TO THE OUTSIDE.

ADDITIONAL
NOTES

There is a little booklet that I just love called *My Heart, Christ's Home*.[6] This booklet portrays the Christian life as a house through which Jesus goes, room to room. It challenges us to search each "room" in our hearts as we desire for God to settle down in our hearts and be fully at home (Ephesians 3:17). Both Jesus and God will make their home in us, as we love and obey them.

What area of your heart needs a little cleaning?

In the four sections of this heart, write down the areas of your heart you need to clean.

After you write them, shade the heart in *red*.

What do you see? (Hebrews 10:22, 12:24)

_____

_____

_____

There is forgiveness. Let us live life in that forgiveness. Amen, sister!

Character is always a choice. Develop your character on the inside; then it will flow to the outside.

Let's close today with the words penned by Paul in Colossians 1:20-23. (We will pick back up here tomorrow.) But for now, list the marvelous works God accomplished through Jesus Christ.

_____

_____

_____

Good job today. As Beth Moore says, "Aren't you glad you came to Bible study?" I know I am, and I hope you are, too.

Reflective prayer:
Write your thoughts, convictions, or insights.

_____

_____

_____

[1] James Strong, The New Strong's Exhaustive Concordance of the Bible. John Walvoord and Roy Zuck, The Bible Knowledge Commentary, New Testament (Colorado Springs: Cook Communications Ministries, 1983, 2000), 671.

[2] John Walvoord and Roy Zuck, The Bible Knowledge Commentary, New Testament (Colorado Springs: Cook Communications Ministries, 1983, 2000).

[3] Anders, Holman New Testament Commentary, 283.

[4] Selwyn Hughes, "Every Day with Jesus," Complete in Christ, March/April 2008 (UK: CWR, 2008).

[5] Ibid.

[6] Robert Munger, My Heart, Christ's Home (Downers Grove, IL: InterVarsity Press, 1986).

Day Four
The Secret is Out

Dear sister, the central dynamic of the Christian life is not what we have done for Christ, but what He has done for us.

Read Colossians 1:21-23 and Ephesians 2:3-6, 12-13. What do these Scriptures convey that our state was prior to our salvation through Christ?

_____

_____

_____

What do these Scriptures convey that Christ did for us?

_____

_____

_____

ADDITIONAL
NOTES

Paul tells us we were enemies in two ways: First, we were enemies in our minds; second, in our behavior. It wasn't that we just thought wrongly—we also acted wrongly. Despite our opposition to God, He reconciled us through the death of Jesus Christ.

In my research, I read that these verses can be divided as follows: what you once were, where you now stand, and how you must go.[1]

Write your own story as you think of these three areas:

What you once were

_____

_____

_____

Where you now stand

_____

_____

_____

How you must go

_____

_____

_____

WOW, if that doesn't put it plainly! Every time I look back at where I have come from, it saddens me—but only for a moment. I realized some years ago that if I got stuck in the "what you once were" stage, I would not move on with God. It also reminds me that I never want to go back to that stage. I want to remain content with the gospel that brought me to Christ. Once we are united with Christ, we can produce good fruit—that is, good deeds for Christ (Romans 7:4).

There is a man in the Old Testament by the name of Enoch. I always wished there was more about him in the Scriptures, but I guess God gave us just what He wanted us to know about him.

Read Genesis 5:21-24 and Hebrews 11:5. Identify those facts you read regarding Enoch.

_____

_____

_____

_____

Enoch's name in Hebrew means "dedicated." In the NLT it states that Enoch enjoyed a close relationship with God throughout his life.[2] Ladies, isn't that what we are striving for? God not only wants a personal relationship with us, but an intimate relationship with each one of us. Our prayer should be, "Draw me closer, Lord Jesus!"

As we continue to look at Paul's work on behalf of the cross of Christ, we may get a little confused when we read Colossians 1:24: "Now I rejoice in what was suffered for you, and I fill up in my flesh what is still lacking in regard to Christ's afflictions, for the sake of his body, which is the church." This suffering that Paul was feeling allowed him to both suffer on behalf of others and identify with Christ. The *Bible Knowledge New Testament Commentary* says, "By this Paul did not mean that Christ's suffering on the cross was insufficient. Paul was not speaking of salvation but of service. Christ's suffering alone procures salvation. But it is a believer's privilege to suffer for Christ."[3]

Read Romans 5:3-4 and James 1:12. What do to these Scriptures say about suffering and trials?

_____

_____

_____

_____

Share a recent trial that God has used to build your character.

_____

_____

_____

_____

BLESSED IS THE
ONE WHO
PERSEVERES
UNDER TRIAL
BECAUSE,
HAVING STOOD
THE TEST, THAT
PERSON WILL
RECEIVE THE
CROWN OF LIFE
THAT THE LORD
HAS PROMISED
TO THOSE WHO
LOVE HIM.

—JAMES 1:12

I want to take a moment to share a trial that God has used in my life to build my character. When I was 27 years old, I battled Cushing's syndrome, a life-threatening disease that confined me to multiple hospital stays for close to four months. Since that day, I have had numerous surgeries to treat the disease. Was it hard? Did I want to give up some days? You bet I did. Looking back over these difficult years, however, I realize how this physical trial has helped to shape me into who I am today. It has brought much glory to the name of Jesus, and others have been drawn closer to Him through my testimony.

If you allow God to teach you valuable lessons as you journey through the trials and are determined to be the best learner you can be, He will turn your life story into a testimony that brings Him much glory.

What was Paul's ministry, and what was his attitude, according to Colossians 1:25?

_____

_____

_____

This verse gives us the answer to what constitutes a God-given ministry: *having a servant's heart.* There are many definitions of servanthood, but recently I read one that drove the point home for me: "becoming excited about making other people successful."[4] When we serve others with a heart filled by Christ, we won't care who receives the glory.

Okay, now we are getting to the portion in Colossians that really hit me and put the burning desire in my heart to pen this study. I just thought it was so cool to realize, *God has a secret.* I was so intrigued with this secret that I wanted to share it with you.

We are going to land here for the remainder of the day. Hopefully when we are finished, you will want to share a secret that is not gossip.

 Read Colossians 1:26-27. What is this mystery "secret"?

_____

_____

_____

Paul calls the message he is responsible to announce, a mystery. Mystery, in the Greek, is *musterion*, which means "a secret; something that was hidden for generations."

The secret is **Jesus Christ!** The secret is not *that* the Gentiles would be saved, for the Old Testament gives evidence of that (Isaiah 49:6), but how *they* could be "fellow-heirs." In Paul's day, this was a revolutionary idea—that the believing Jews and Gentiles could be joined together as one.

> **Read Ephesians 2:12-14, 3:6-7, and Galatians 3:28-29. Write how these truths have had an impact on you.**

_____

_____

_____

_____

_____

_____

_____

Dear sister, so many of us don't live as though we truly are God's children. If we really understood the depth of our sonship with God, would we live differently?

Read Romans 8:15-17. Who are we heirs with?

_____

_____

Too little is made of the inheritance that we have received as children of God. We may not be able to enjoy much of this inheritance until we get to heaven, but we will be able to enjoy some of it in the here and now.

In the NASB, Psalm 16:6 says, "The lines have fallen to me in pleasant places. Indeed, my heritage is beautiful to me." In this psalm, David speaks of the joys and benefits of a life lived in companionship with God. He compared God's blessings to the best inheritance a person could receive in the present. The Lord had truly given him a wonderful, full life.

Look up these Scriptures and match them with God's truths:

Psalm 27:13   I will see the goodness of the Lord in the land of the living.

Psalm 116:9   You are my place of refuge. You are all I really want in life.

Psalm 142:5   And so I walk in the Lord's presence as I live here on earth.

In Jeremiah 3:19, God's desire was to give them a beautiful inheritance and desirable land, but the Israelites turned away from following their Father.

God wants to give us blessings as we walk this journey with Him here on planet Earth, continuing to seek Him and obey His instruction and not turn away from Him. Enjoying His permanent presence is a gift in itself.

ADDITIONAL NOTES

Read Ecclesiastes 5:19. What practical gift has God given to us?

_____

_____

_____

Are you viewing what God has given you, whether much or little, with the right perspective? Are you accepting your lot or condition in life? Our possessions should not be the source of our joy but a reason to rejoice, since every good thing comes from God.

Do you have great needs or are you discontented because you don't have what you want? Why?

_____

_____

_____

_____

_____

_____

EVERY GOOD
AND PERFECT
GIFT IS
FROM ABOVE,
COMING
DOWN FROM
THE FATHER
OF THE
HEAVENLY
LIGHTS, WHO
DOES NOT
CHANGE LIKE
SHIFTING
SHADOWS.

—JAMES 1:17

As we close today, oh, that we would remember that God is the greatest gift-giver as He chooses to whom He gives and from whom He takes away. When I finally accepted this concept in my life, it changed my thinking about why I didn't have something that someone else may have had or why He hadn't fulfilled what I thought He had called me to. If you are like me, at times you want to hurry God along in His process. But through the waiting, ladies, I came to know God in a deeper way. He showed me more about Himself, and I realized that the preparation time was necessary for this season of my life. One thing I know is that we are always learning more about Him as we journey, so we should enjoy the present, for today is a gift in itself.

Reflective prayer:
Write your thoughts, convictions, or insights.

_____

_____

_____

_____

[1] Selwyn Hughes, "Every Day with Jesus," Complete in Christ, March/April 2008 (UK: CWR, 2008).

[2] Life Application Study Bible, New Living Translation.

[3] Anders, Holman New Testament Commentary.

[4] Selwyn Hughes, "Every Day with Jesus," Complete in Christ, March/April 2008 (UK: CWR, 2008).

ADDITIONAL NOTES

ENJOY THE PRESENT, FOR TODAY IS A GIFT IN ITSELF.

Day Five
Ministry is Hard Work

As we close chapter 1 of Colossians, we will unpack the real truth that authentic ministry is tough work. Paul made this very clear by calling his ministry labor.

 Read Colossians 1:28-29. What did Paul work hard at?

_____

_____

_____

No doubt Paul admonished (warned) and taught (educated) everyone about Jesus due to the false teaching about Christ in Colossae. In counseling and instructing the Colossian believers, Paul knew it is the truth about the power of the gospel and the person of Christ that is the believer's best protection against deception.

We can learn to recognize false teachers in the same way a banker detects counterfeit currency: by studying the genuine article. If we devote ourselves to studying the genuine article, which is the truth of the Scriptures, then we don't need to know the particulars of the false teachers we may come across. An intimate knowledge of the Word of God is the only defense we need against the deception of the world's religions.[1]

GO DEEPER

Read Proverbs 1:7, 9:10, 15:33 and Ecclesiastes 12:13.

What have you learned about knowledge from these Scriptures?

_____

_____

_____

Dear sister, wisdom begins with knowing God. He gives insight into right living. To know God, you can't just know the facts about Him. Instead, you must have a personal, intimate relationship with Him. If you really want to be wise, get to know God better and better.

What does James 1:5 tell us to do if we want wisdom?

_____

_____

_____

Now, that seems way too simple—*to just ask for it.* Yes, God is willing to give us the wisdom, but our goals cannot be self-centered. Rather, they must be God-centered. The more we get into the Word, the better we'll understand God's will. We will need to be deliberate about what God tells us and then be obedient to His will.

How often do you meet with God?

_____ Daily _____ Weekly _____ Monthly

_____ If in Need _____ Occasionally

What does this reveal to you about your relationship with Him?

_____

_____

_____

What changes will you have to make to enjoy a more intimate relationship with God?

_____

_____

_____

Read 2 Timothy 3:16-17 and Romans 15:4.
How is God's Word useful?

_____

_____

God will equip us when we get into His Word. Not only is His Word informing us, but it is also transforming us. It is timeless and true. Our knowledge of God's Word should strengthen our faith and lead us to want to do good works. If not, it is not useful. God already knows what it is going to take to make us more like His Son. So, the more we are in His Word, the more He will reveal Himself to us (John 14:21).

What do you believe Paul's goal was, according to Colossians 1:28?

_____

_____

_____

In the Greek, "perfect" *(teleion)* means "mature or complete."[2] It doesn't mean without blemish. Paul was interested in believers not remaining spiritual babies but becoming spiritually mature.

In 1 Corinthians 3:1-3, Paul shares the proof of the Corinthians' infancy. What do you learn from this passage about being a baby Christian?

_____

_____

_____

List the areas in your own life where you need to become mature.

_____

_____

_____

While studying this passage from The Life Application Bible (NLT), I read this accompanying note: Being controlled by our own desires will stunt our growth![3] I thought, OUCH! I wondered where I would be today if I hadn't followed my own ways most of the time. Ladies, I pray that we would mature in our walk with God so that He would be recognizable to others around us, and we would become more perfect in our relationship with Him.

 Whose mighty power does Paul rely on, according to Colossians 1:29?

_____

The Amplified Version expresses it like this: "For this I labor [unto weariness], striving with all the superhuman energy which He so mightily enkindles and works within me." Paul's labor did not depend on human energy, but the power that comes from Christ. Paul lived by using all the energy Christ generated within him. As he did, Christ added His energy as well to make him able to do more than he could ever imagine.

Is there something you are working on so hard to accomplish for God? Who are you relying on—yourself, or God?

_____

There are times we go about our own way, doing ministry for God but not with Him. Have you ever done something for God and only asked Him to go into the meeting or the event with you sixty seconds before you enter? What is wrong with this picture? Who are we relying on?

ADDITIONAL NOTES

KNOWING GOD'S WORD, DESIRING GOD'S WORD, AND LOVING GOD'S WORD IS WHAT TRANSFORMS OUR INNER BEING.

Dear sister, we shouldn't just prepare ourselves physically (logistics) and mentally (what to say). We also need to prepare ourselves spiritually. Then, the physical and mental preparation will flow from the spiritual foundation. I am so thankful for the men and women whom God has brought into my life to teach me, just when I needed them to challenge and encourage my motives and dreams. In other words, we are not meant to minister alone, but together.

> • Knowing God's Word,
> • Desiring God's Word, and
> • Loving God's Word
>   is what transforms our inner being.

Go Deeper

Read 1 Corinthians 9:25 and 2 Timothy 2:1-6.

List the types of people Paul uses as illustrations to emphasize his point about hard labor.

_____

_____

_____

There is no doubt that ministry is hard work. Like Paul, we should desire to equip others for God's work with a heart to develop and add value to them as we serve them. Are you willing to endure anything if it will bring salvation, with eternal glory in Christ Jesus, to those God has chosen (2 Timothy 2:10)?

I appreciate your diligence in completing the first week of work and pray it has been enlightening for you.

Reflective prayer:

Write your thoughts, convictions, or insights.

_____

_____

_____

_____

_____

_____

[1] Anders, Holman New Testament Commentary, 286.

[2] Strong, The New Strong's Exhaustive Concordance of the Bible, 71.

[3] Life Application Study Bible, New Living Translation, 1804.

Week One
Video Session

Colossians
Week Two

Day One
Our Treasure is Christ

Day Two
Christ is Enough

Day Three
A Heart of Flesh

Day Four
You are Forgiven

Day Five
To Judge or Not to Judge

Day One
Our Treasure is Christ

In chapter 1, Paul established the supremacy of Christ. Christ is God Himself in human flesh. Now in chapter 2, the apostle confronts the false teachings that were threatening to lead not only the Colossian believers astray, but also their sister church in Laodicea.

In Colossians 2:1, Paul shares that he struggles. In the Greek, *agon* means that he "had concern and anxiety."[1]

Paul was not in prison because he struggled. No, this was an intense inner struggle on behalf of the believers in Colossae and Laodicea, as well as those who had not met him personally. Paul recognized false teaching and wanted nothing more for the Colossians than to be aware of the deceptive damage it could bring.

GO DEEPER

Read Acts 20:28-31, Romans 16:17-18, Galatians 1:6-9, 1 Timothy 1:3-7, and 6:3-5.

What do the warnings in these verses have to say about false teachers?

_____

_____

_____

When false teachers appear to know the Bible, their influence can be dangerously subtle. So, how can we recognize false teaching? Ask yourself these questions.

- Does the teaching promote controversy rather than unity?
- Does the teaching help others come to Jesus?
- Is their motivation to make a name for themselves?
- Is their motivation to gain honor and prestige?
- Is it contrary to the true teaching of the Scriptures?

Again, dear sister, the best way to detect false teachers in our day is to know the truth itself. Study, read, and understand the depths of the greatest book ever sold. It is in your hands—the written Word of God, our Bible!

Read Colossians 2:2-3. What was the goal Paul had in mind for the Colossians?

_____

_____

_____

Not much has changed since Paul wrote this book to the Colossians in AD 60. He wanted them, and us, to be encouraged (strengthened). That takes place as believers are united together in love, and that unity creates strength. A person left alone is much more vulnerable than a cohesive unit.

When we are united in love, we will be strengthened in heart. Then we will have assurance for understanding one another. We need to have one mind as well as one heart.

Read Ecclesiastes 4:9-12. What does this Scripture say regarding companionship?

_____

_____

_____

 Read Colossians 2:3-5. What is hidden in Christ?

_____

_____

_____

Paul reinforces that wisdom and knowledge are hidden in Christ alone because the false teachers taught they are hidden away in mystical experiences and higher knowledge. Indeed, Christ is all we need!

Ladies, don't look for treasure that you already have. Christ is our treasure—our gift from God and our fullness of Him—so we have been given this fullness. Do we treat Him as our treasure, or do we take Him for granted?

Paul told the believers about the hidden treasures of wisdom and knowledge because he didn't want them to go on a wild goose chase. God doesn't want us to be deceived, either.

Read Acts 17:10-15 and 1 Timothy 6:20-21. How do these verses instruct us to emulate Timothy and the Bereans?

_____

_____

_____

Though error was threatening the churches of Colossae and Laodicea, Paul was encouraged by their order and firm faith (2:5). So, yes, it is possible to be in the world and not of the world. When we are in Him, we are in good order; outside of Him, we are in disorder.

Is there an area in your life that is out of order? If so, what do you need to do to get it back into order?

_____

_____

_____

_____

_____

_____

After giving them words of encouragement, Paul goes on to exhort his readers to not only receive Him, but to continue to live (walk) in Him. Paul's desire is for the believers to understand that receiving Him is just the beginning. To continue to build on their foundation, they must follow Christ daily.

GO DEEPER

Read Colossians 2:6-7, Ephesians 4:1-3, and 1 John 2:6. According to these Scriptures, who should our "walk" resemble and what should it look like?

_____

_____

_____

To walk today as Christ did, we must obey His teachings and follow His example of complete obedience to God. Step by step and day by day, we should conduct ourselves in conscious submission to the lordship of Jesus Christ.

What we believe is always evident in our lives, and evidence is the proof of our inner belief. Who we are on the inside will spill over onto our outside for all to see.

How often does your lifestyle reflect your obedience to God by the way you "walk" through life?

___ Once in a while   ___ When you need it to   ___ Not usually

___ Daily

Re-read Colossians 2:7. What are the benefits of being rooted in Christ?

_____

_____

_____

We are not supposed to be like tumbleweeds without a root system, blown around by every wind of doctrine. Roots don't exist for themselves; instead, they exist to give the plant nourishment and strength to help it grow.[2] This is why we must be firmly rooted in Jesus Christ—so we can continue to grow in our faith and overflow with thanksgiving.

Rooted in Him = growth in Him; established in Him = built up in Him. The final test involves showing how thankful we are. Take a moment to thank God for your life and His provision for your daily needs. He is truly worthy of our thanksgiving!

_____

_____

_____

Let's close today with a final reading from Ephesians 3:14-19. Underline the benefits of the glorious love of God when we are rooted in Him.

> For this reason, I kneel before the Father, from whom his whole family in heaven and on earth derives its name. I pray that out of his glorious riches he may strengthen you with power through his Spirit in your inner being, so that Christ may dwell in your hearts through faith. And I pray that you, being rooted and established in love, may have power, together with all the saints, to grasp how wide and long and high and deep is the love of Christ, and to know this love that surpasses knowledge—that you may be filled to the measure of all the fullness of God.

Pray this for yourself and your loved ones.

TO BE ROOTED
IN CHRIST
MEANS GROWTH
IN CHRIST.
TO BE
ESTABLISHED IN
CHRIST MEANS
TO BE BUILT UP
IN CHRIST.

Reflective prayer:

Write your thoughts, convictions, or insights.

_____

_____

_____

_____

_____

_____

[1] Holman New Testament Commentary; Galatians, Ephesians, Philippians, Colossians. Nashville, TN: Broadman & Holman,1999, 302.

[2] Anders, Holman New Testament Commentary, 304

ADDITIONAL NOTES

Day Two
Christ is Enough

Philosophy originally had a good meaning: "the love of wisdom." By the first century, however, this word pertained to almost any speculations about God, as well as the world and life in general, including those based on occult and human tradition.[1]

According to Colossians 2:8, what type of philosophy are we to be aware of?

_____

_____

_____

Paul's concern for the Colossians here is that they must not allow themselves to be kidnapped by an empty deception based on human ideas and defeated spirit beings. Referring to false teachers and their philosophies, Eugene Peterson translates this phrase, "They spread their lies through the empty traditions of human beings and the empty superstitions of spirit beings" (MSG).

Can you name some philosophies or worldly traditions Christians should be aware of today?

_____

_____

_____

Paul is a philosopher himself, so he is not condemning philosophy in and of itself. Instead, he is condemning any human teaching that does not include Christ as the answer to life's problems.

There is only one way we can stand firm against these "giants" of false teachers: by wearing the full armor of God.

Read Ephesians 6:10-18. Describe the pieces of armor we will need to put on.

_____

_____

_____

We must use this spiritual armor to RESIST the Devil's schemes, not to attack him. At times, the spiritual warfare in which we find ourselves may be frightening. However, the only thing we have to fear, if we have our armor on, is fear itself. "The one who is in you (Jesus) is greater than the one (Satan) who is in the world" (1 John 4:4).

We need to understand this spiritual armor in order to best handle our daily combat against the false teachings of the world system in which we live.

The belt of truth – We accept the truth of the Bible and choose to follow it with integrity. When we do this, we will arm ourselves with truth and not the fallacies that come from others.

The breastplate of righteousness – In our striving to be Christlike, we live according to His ways of righteousness, which protect our heart. We let our head knowledge of the Scriptures become our breastplate that protects our heart from Satan's schemes.

Our feet fitted with the readiness – We need to believe the promises of God in the gospel and count on them to be true. This will keep us steadfast in Christ and standing firm against lies that come at us.

The shield of faith – This shield will deflect the blows from the swords and arrows of the Enemy and help us reject those temptations to doubt and sin. As we build upon our faith daily, we will be shielded by God.

The helmet of salvation – This helmet will help protect our minds. We will need to rest on our trust and hope in the future while living in this world according to the values of heaven.

The Sword of the Spirit – The Word of the Lord. We will need to use the Scriptures specifically in life's situations to fend off attacks of the Enemy, just as Jesus did when He was tempted by the Devil in the wilderness (Matthew 4:1-11).

ADDITIONAL NOTES

The Scriptures are utterly consistent regarding spiritual warfare. If we have our armor in place and stand firm in our faith, we may resist the Devil and his empty philosophies. If we do, the Devil will flee from us (James 4:7).

The only part of our bodies not covered by the armor of God is our back. This is another reason we will need other believers to gather around and stand alongside of us. When we stand back to back with our sisters and brothers in Christ, we will be better protected from the Enemy.

Read Colossians 2:9-10 and answer the following questions:

What lives in Christ?

_____

In what type of form?

_____

What have we been given?

_____

Who is the Lord over all the universe?

_____

GO DEEPER

 We must continue to discover the truths about our fullness in Christ. What do John 1:16, Ephesians 3:19 and 4:12-13 tell us?

_____

_____

_____

Because of our vital union with Jesus, the Full One, believers have been given fullness (completeness) in Christ. This fullness involves the working power of the inner strength supplied by the Holy Spirit, which leads to the indwelling of Christ, then to His abundant love, and finally to God's fullness in us. The only way this infilling will be complete in us is through our constant pursuit of Him, all the while praying for Him to strengthen us with the power of His Spirit. It will be His presence, His power, His love, and His life that will inhabit us and complete us!

Outside of Jesus, there is only emptiness. Christ is enough! As philosopher Jean Paul Sartre puts it, "Life is an empty bubble on the sea of nothingness."[2] Are you trying to fill areas in your life with "somethingness" besides Jesus? If so, are you coming up empty?

What areas in your life do you need to allow God to fill?

_____

_____

_____

_____

ADDITIONAL NOTES

"I AM THE VINE; YOU ARE THE BRANCHES. IF YOU REMAIN IN ME AND I IN YOU, YOU WILL BEAR MUCH FRUIT; APART FROM ME YOU CAN DO NOTHING."

—JOHN 15:5

In my early years as a believer, I looked for Christ in all the wrong areas. I thought friends, material gains, and yes, even love could fulfill me. But the more I read His Word, the more I fell in love with the Giver of life and realized that apart from Him, I could do nothing. Dear sister, it is futile to look for spiritual fulfillment or maturity in any other place than Jesus Christ, who is the treasure house of all wisdom and knowledge and fullness of deity.

Finish today strong with this reading from 1 John 4:1-6. How can you detect false teachers who don't believe that Jesus is fully God and fully man?

_____

_____

_____

The truth of the matter is that the full deity of Christ is, nonetheless, in bodily form!

Reflective prayer:
Write your thoughts, convictions, or insights.

_____

_____

_____

[1] Suzie Klein, Disciplers Bible Studies: Colossians, Lesson three (Palos Verdes Estates, CA, 2001), 2.

[2] John Walvoord and Roy Zuck, The Bible Knowledge Commentary: New Testament, 677.

Day Three

Day Three
A Heart of Flesh

In Colossians 2:11-12, Paul chooses to explain our full salvation through the metaphors of **circumcision** and **baptism.** The point of these metaphors is that we are saved totally and exclusively through the work of God, not through any human activity.[1]

Begin by reading Colossians 2:11-12 for yourself. Then let's break the passage down to better understand these two powerful acts.

When we came to Christ, what did we have (v. 11)?

_____

According to this specific verse, what does it mean to be circumcised?

_____

Was this procedure spiritual or physical?

_____

Additional Notes
ADDITIONAL NOTES

ADDITIONAL
NOTES

According to verse 12, what does baptism mean?

_____

GO DEEPER

_NO_ religious ritual can make us alive with Christ. In the old covenant, however, the ancient Jews were masters at performing physical rites in their efforts to maintain their relationship with God. **According to the following verses, what does circumcision signify?**

Genesis 17:9-11

_____

Deuteronomy 10:16, 30:6

_____

Jeremiah 4:4

_____

Ezekiel 44:7, 9

_____

It becomes more unmistakable in the New Testament that the circumcision Paul is talking about in Colossians 2 is the spiritual operation of cutting away the "sinful nature."

 Read Romans 2:28-29 and 4:9-13 in the New Living Translation. What is "true" circumcision, according to these passages? _(See side bar.)_

_____

_____

_____

[28]For you are not a true Jew just because you were born of Jewish parents or because you have gone through the ceremony of circumcision. [29]No, a true Jew is one whose heart is right with God. And true circumcision is not merely obeying the letter of the law; rather, it is a change of heart produced by God's Spirit. And a person with a changed heart seeks praise[a] from God, not from people.

(Romans 2:28-29 NLT)

So, true circumcision involves a change of heart by God's Spirit. This is an operation only God can perform; indeed, no human surgery can cut out your sinful nature. No matter how impure your life may seem right now, you can have a new nature when you ask Christ to reign in your heart. God offers you a fresh start and will give you a new heart for Him. (See "Christ in Your Heart," page 225, to learn about Christ's reign in your life.) You will become holy only when you choose to be a slave to righteousness, putting off the sinful nature, or the "old man" (Romans 6:6 NKJV) and deliberately putting on the new nature.

Read Ezekiel 36:25-27 and 2 Corinthians 5:17. What does Christ provide for you?

_____

_____

_____

Have you allowed the Great Surgeon to perform the necessary changes in your life? Be specific.

_____

_____

_____

We were in Adam—sinful, fallen, and corrupt—so we were dead in our sins. Through Jesus Christ's sacrificial death on the cross, however, the power of death over us was completely destroyed. Dear sister, new life begins at the moment of salvation when we are spiritually baptized into Jesus Christ.

[9]Now, is this blessing only for the Jews, or is it also for uncircumcised Gentiles?[a] Well, we have been saying that Abraham was counted as righteous by God because of his faith. [10]But how did this happen? Was he counted as righteous only after he was circumcised, or was it before he was circumcised? Clearly, God accepted Abraham before he was circumcised!

[11] Circumcision was a sign that Abraham already had faith and that God had already accepted him and declared him to be righteous—even before he was circumcised. So Abraham is the spiritual father of those who have faith but have not been circumcised. They are counted as righteous because of their faith. [12]And Abraham is also the spiritual father of those who have been circumcised, but only if they have the same kind of faith Abraham had before he was circumcised.

[13]Clearly, God's promise to give the whole earth to Abraham and his descendants was based not on his obedience to God's law, but on a right relationship with God that comes by faith.

(Romans 4:9-13 NLT)

GO DEEPER

According to the following Scriptures, what does baptism signify?

Mark 1:4

_____

Romans 6:3-4

_____

1 Corinthians 12:13

_____

Baptism visually represents the death, burial, and resurrection of Christ. Our immersion in water portrays the death and burial of our old sinful ways. Coming out of the water depicts our resurrection by the power of God to "live a new life."

How well are you living your "new life" in Christ?

_____

_____

_____

_____

If you have been walking with Christ for many years, have you become complacent in your life with Him?

_____

_____

_____

Share with your group something "new" God has shown you through this study. How have you been challenged?

_____

_____

_____

_____

Wow, we looked up many verses today. Good job! End today with a prayer of thanksgiving about who YOU are in Christ.

> I'm thanking you, God, from a full heart; I'm writing the book on your wonders.
> I'm whistling, laughing, and jumping for joy; I'm singing your song, High God.
>
> (Psalm 9:1-2 MSG)

Reflective prayer:

Write your thoughts, convictions, or insights.

_____

_____

_____

_____

[1] Anders, Holman New Testament Commentary, 306

Day Four
You are Forgiven

As we continue to look at spiritual fullness, we will see that the reality of forgiveness is found in Jesus Christ.

Read Colossians 2:13-15. What did God do for you when you were dead in your transgressions?

_____

_____

_____

God has made us alive with Christ. When His life pulses through our souls, then freedom from sin is possible. Not only has God made us alive with Christ, but He has also cancelled the written code that was against us by nailing it to the cross.

New life came when we accepted Christ as our Savior and God forgave us of all our sins. For more on forgiveness, let's . . .

ADDITIONAL NOTES

GO DEEPER

From the following verses, what do you learn about sin and forgiveness?

Romans 6:6-11

_____

_____

_____

1 Peter 2:24-25

_____

_____

_____

1 John 1:9

_____

_____

_____

In Colossians 2:14, Paul speaks of a written code with regulations, which stands against us and is opposed to us. The Law was like a handwritten "certificate of debt" (NASB) or a signed confession of guilt that stood as a perpetual witness against a debtor. It is the Greek term for an IOU.

In Colossians 2:14, what did Paul say God did with this IOU?

_____

The word "cancelled" *(exaleipho)* means "to sponge; wipe off; erase."[1] This is what Christ has done with ALL our sins. The written code that condemned us has been sponged off by the blood of Christ—as if it had never been.

God erased your debt. What does this truth do for you?

_____

_____

_____

From these verses, we also see that not only did God erase our debt, but He also took it away and nailed it to the cross. When Jesus died, the condemning document was DESTROYED!

YOU are fully forgiven. At times, it may seem hard to accept this forgiveness because of past regrets—thoughts that seem to pop up out of nowhere or periods of just downright rebellion. During these times when Satan tries to manipulate your thoughts and desires, you need to CHOOSE to believe you are forgiven and trust His truths. You will need to replace any lies with truths from God's Word.

Read Luke 7:36-50, the story of the sinful woman.

What acts did the woman perform to show her gratitude toward Christ?

_____

_____

_____

Compare Simon with the sinful woman. Discuss each one's actions or the lack thereof.

_____

_____

_____

What is the point of Jesus' story (v. 47)?

_____

_____

_____

Dear sister, this sinful woman went from feeling shame to feeling chosen. That is exactly what Jesus can do for us. When we realize the depth of our sinfulness, we will begin to appreciate the complete forgiveness God can offer. Overflowing love will naturally flow from us with gratitude and demonstrations of faith.

Since we have been forgiven so much, how should we respond to God's forgiveness?

Read Matthew 6:14-15. What will happen if we don't forgive others?

_____

Spiritual fullness means complete salvation, full forgiveness, and absolute victory. Christ experienced true victory on the cross.

As early as Genesis 3:15, the Scriptures mention that a conqueror would come to crush the head of the serpent.

Match the following Scriptures with the attempts of Satan to destroy Christ.

Luke 23:6-12   Satan attempts to destroy Jesus with his own temptation in the wilderness. (Unsuccessful)

Matthew 4:1-11   Satan attempts to destroy Jesus through the efforts of Herod. (Unsuccessful)

Now read John 3:14-15 and 12:31-33. How would Jesus gain the victory over Satan?

_____

On the cross Jesus consummated His victory. The purpose of His death was to defeat Satan and his evil league through the forgiveness of sins. On the cross, Jesus won a decisive victory, settling forever that Satan is a vanquished foe. Yes, the Devil has been defeated, but because he has not yet conceded to the defeat, he will continue to harass us. As we continue to learn about our identity in Christ, however, we can live above Satan's control.

Read 1 John 4:4. How can we overcome the world?

_____

_____

_____

Is there something you are struggling to overcome? Have you been battling it for too long? Have you allowed God to take control? Have you taken your hands off the wheel and let God be the driver? Think about who's in control of your life. Temptation comes when we're lured by our own evil desires (James 1:14).

I have had to overcome some difficult situations and people in my own life. It was only when I let God occupy my thoughts and deeds that I was able to defeat those temptations. Sometimes it happens minute by minute, but I promise that if you start with the minutes, it will turn into hours . . . then days . . . then into months and years. What was once a temptation that overcame you will then fade into a distant memory, conquered by the victory you have in Jesus Christ.

During retreats I've held, I pray a poem called "Start Over" by Woodrow Kroll.[2] This may be what some of you need to do: clean your slate and begin anew.

> When you've trusted Jesus and walked his way
> When you've felt his hand lead you day by day
> But your steps now take you another way,
> START OVER.
>
> When you've made your plans and they've gone awry
> When you've tried your best and there's no more try
> When you've failed yourself and you don't know why,
> START OVER.
>
> When you've told your friends what you plan to do
> When you've trusted them and they didn't come through
> And now you're all alone and it's up to you,
> START OVER.
>
> When you've failed your kids and they're grown and gone
> When you've done your best but it's turned out wrong
> And now your grandchildren have come along,
> START OVER.
>
> When you've prayed to God so you'll know his will
> When you've prayed and prayed and you don't know still

When you want to stop 'cause you've had your fill,
START OVER.

When you think you're finished and want to quit
When you've bottomed out in life's deepest pit
When you've tried and tried to get out of it,
START OVER.

When the year has been long and successes few
When December comes and you're feeling blue
God gives a January just for you,
START OVER.

Starting over means "Victories Won"
Starting over means "A Race Well Run"
Starting over means "The Lord's Will Done"
Don't just sit there . . . Start over
START OVER.

Reflective prayer:
Write your thoughts, convictions, or insights.

_____

_____

_____

_____

_____

[1] Selwyn Hughes, "Every Day with Jesus," Complete in Christ, March/
April 2008 (UK: CWR, 2008).

[2] Woodrow Kroll, "Turning Back to God," www.turnbacktogod.com/
poem-start-over, (2 April 2011).

ADDITIONAL NOTES

Day Five
To Judge or Not to Judge

Yesterday from our reading, we saw the triumph Jesus had over every power and authority that raged against Him. In light of this, Paul will now encourage the Colossian believers to celebrate Christ's victory in a life free from unnecessary rituals and ceremonies.

Read Colossians 2:16-17.

What should we not allow others to do?

_____

What are all these things a shadow of?

_____

We need to know that we must not allow others to intimidate us or question our spirituality. I know this was convicting for me. I find myself sometimes on the other side, as the one who passes judgment. Let's see what God's Word says about judging others.

GO DEEPER

Read the following Scriptures and identify what each one reveals about judging.

Matthew 7:1-2, 4

_____

_____

_____

1 Corinthians 4:5

_____

_____

_____

James 4:11-12

_____

_____

_____

Ouch! This type of judging, tearing another down rather than building another up, is a hypocritical, critical attitude—one that we will want to stay clear away from. God will be the final judge, not us (1 Corinthians 4:3-5)!

Judge – form an opinion or conclusion about
  • When we judge, we will want to make sure we gather all the facts before acting.

Criticize – find fault with

- We will want to be careful of a "habitually critical" spirit. The antonym for "criticize" is "praise." So when you feel like criticizing someone, break into praise over that person instead.

Does this mean that we should overlook wrong behavior within the church body? No, we cannot allow our sisters and brothers in Christ to keep on sinning and thus damage the reputation of the church. Our goal for approaching our fellow Christians in sin is to reconcile them back to God, not to condemn them.

Read Matthew 18:15-17. List the steps you should take with another believer if they are sinning.

_____

_____

_____

Okay, I got off on a bunny trail, but it was a good path to take. I know I needed to be reminded of my attitude. I hope you gleaned from it, too.

Let's return to Colossians 2:16-17. It was clear that the false teachers of Paul's day were trying to make people believe that Christ's sacrifice and His indwelling presence within the believer were not enough to achieve holiness. According to them, other matters such as New Moon celebrations or Sabbath day rituals were also essential. In the same way, we should not let others condemn us for eating certain foods or drinking specific beverages, or whether or not we participate in particular religious festivals.

To better understand what Christ says about what is acceptable, discuss what is truly important to God, according to these verses.

Mark 7:14-23

_____

_____

_____

Acts 10:9-16

_____

_____

_____

Romans 14:17

_____

_____

_____

Do you worry more about what is in your diet, or what is in your heart and mind? In the Old Testament the Jews believed that they could be cleansed/purified before God by what they refused to eat (Leviticus 11). Yet Jesus makes it clear that sin actually begins in the heart. We are pure, not because of our outward acts, but as a result of the inward work of Jesus Christ, which transforms us to be more like Him.

The ceremonial rules put forth in the Law were merely a shadow of things to come (Colossians 2:17). A shadow is an inferior, rough image that is cast by a real, substantial object. When one finds the real object, the shadow is no longer needed.[1] The reality is Jesus Christ. Those who have found Christ no longer need to follow the shadow—the laws of the Old Testament. If we have Christ, we have all that we need to know and please God.

What, if anything, keeps you from living free in Christ? Is there a ritual or man-made rule that has you imprisoned?

_____

_____

_____

Paul has given the Colossians many warnings in this chapter, and he continues to point out more in verses 18 and 19.

What warnings do you see in these two verses?

_____

_____

_____

Many commentators believe that one aspect of the heresy threatening the church in that day was the worship of angels—the false doctrine of seeking out mediators in addition to Christ. We all have our own perception of angels, but let's see what the Word of God says.

GO DEEPER

What do the following verses tell us about angels?

Exodus 20:3-4

_____

ADDITIONAL
NOTES

_____

_____

Psalm 91:11-12

_____

_____

_____

Hebrews 1:14

_____

_____

_____

Revelation 22:8-9

_____

_____

_____

It is important to know that you should never call on an angel for guidance, deliverance, etc. To do so would only open yourself up to spiritual deception. According to the Bible, we should ONLY call on God. While it is true that He might deliver us using angels, it is still God alone who is our Rock, Fortress, and Deliverer. God commands His angels what to do, and they obey Him.

The root of the trouble in Colossae involved those puffed up with pride who advocated the worship of angels. Ladies, either pride must die in us or Christ cannot live in us.

The second warning to the Colossians was not to lose their connection with the Head (v. 19). Without a vital link to the Head, the body of Christ cannot grow. Growth comes not from men, but only from God. Aggressive methods and strong appeals can add numbers to a church, but only God can make a church grow.

Describe the parallel image to the headship of Christ found in John 15:5.

_____

_____

_____

As we close this week, read Colossians 2:20-23. What kinds of things appear to be wise but are of no value, according to this passage?

_____

_____

_____

Dear sister, we are not governed by rules, but by our relationship with Jesus. We are not saved by what we do, but by what Christ has done. Knowing the truth that fullness, forgiveness, and freedom are found in Jesus should strengthen us against attractive but empty deception.

Paul tells us that asceticism (a man-made system of rules) is all appearance and thus of no value! He says this kind of behavior has no value in restraining sensual indulgence. To put it plainly, all this external performance has no effect on internal urges. Alexander Maclaren, a nineteenth-century Baptist teacher, said, "There is only one thing that will put the collar on the neck of the animal inside of us, and that is the

ADDITIONAL
NOTES

power of the indwelling Christ."[2] When we acknowledge that Jesus has unlimited power because He's a limitless God, He not only gives us the Holy Spirit to fight against the flesh, but He also gives us new desires as well. We simply need to yield to HIM!

This was a long day, but I hope it was worth the study. Press on, dear sister.

Reflective prayer:
Write your thoughts, convictions, or insights.

_____

_____

_____

_____

_____

[1] Klein, Disciplers Bible Studies: Colossians.
[2] Anders, Holman New Testament Commentary, 310.

Week Two
Video Session

Colossians
Week Three

Day One
He is Your Life!

Day Two
A Transformed Lifestyle is the
Trademark of a New Life

Day Three
Love is the Garment the World Sees;
All Other Virtues are Undergarments

Day Four
A Word to Wives

Day Five
Family Ties

Day One
He is Your Life!

Paul's letter to the Colossians is neatly divided—the first two chapters are doctrinal, and the second half is practical. As we look at Colossians 3 this week, we will examine Paul's discussions about our relationships with Christ, the local church, family, daily work, and unbelievers. He emphasizes that if we don't keep our relationship with Christ intact, all of our other relationships will not succeed.

Let's begin by looking at our relationship with Christ.

Along with Colossians 3:1-4, read Ephesians 2:4-7. Answer the following questions about foundational Christian living.

According to these verses, with whom have Christians been raised?

_____

_____

_____

ADDITIONAL
NOTES

What should Christians set their minds on?

_____

_____

What should Christians not do? Why?

_____

_____

What is our future hope (v. 4)?

_____

_____

In the Greek, the phrase "set your hearts" *(zeteite)*[1] literally means "seek." The broader range of meaning includes "trying to find the location of someone or something; attempting to obtain something." The emphasis of this entire chapter is on the changed lifestyle that should grow out of our identification with Christ.

Dear sister, the way we live is the ultimate test of our maturity. Constant attention must be paid to this changed lifestyle that Paul sets forth.

Where is your mind set? Why?

_____

_____

What/who are you seeking?

_____

_____

What are the things you think about daily? If any changes need to be made, what would they be?

_____

_____

_____

Paul tells us to set our minds on things above. Let's take a glimpse into what the apostle John observed when he was given his vision of heaven.

Read Revelation 4:1-11. What is God worthy of (v. 11)?

_____

_____

_____

In awe of the greatness of God, let us think about His greatness daily as we live for Him—here and now. May our lives produce the "things above," such as compassion, kindness, humility, gentleness, patience, forgiveness, and love (Colossians 3:12-14) as we come in contact with people.

Setting our minds on things above does not mean that we should live in a mystical fog or neglect our affairs in the here and now. What it does mean is that we are not only to be concerned with the trivialities of the temporal, but that we should also view everything (actions and relationships) against the backdrop of eternity. With this new perspective on life, the eternal will surely have an impact on the temporal.[2] Okay, that means we do even the mundane things like cooking dinner and cleaning the house with a better attitude. Oh boy, does that hit home!

ADDITIONAL
NOTES

L OVE
O THERS IN
V IEW OF
E TERNITY

LOVE IS WHAT
WE WILL SHOW
IN OUR LIVES IF
WE HAVE THE
LOVE OF GOD
SHED ABROAD
IN OUR HEARTS.
WE WILL NOT
HAVE TO GO
UP AND DOWN
THE EARTH
PROCLAIMING
IT. WE WILL
SHOW IT IN
EVERYTHING WE
SAY OR DO.

—DWIGHT L. MOODY

When we have eternal love on our minds and hearts, it is easier to love others as God has commanded us to love (John 13:34)!

Is there someone you need to love through the eyes of Jesus?

_____

_____

If so, what can you do to become more loving?

_____

_____

_____

Okay, I know I am being pretty blunt, but John tells us in 1 John 4:11-12 that since God loved us, we ought to love others. Because God lives in us, others see Him by the way we love.

Love God and love others! WOW!

How are you loving others around you? Do you want to display Jesus in a loving way? Then begin to love those who are not very lovable along with those who are. Begin to love others in view of eternity. You will draw others to Jesus by your loving attitude.

Nonetheless, we can only live like this because we are hidden in Christ with God (Colossians 3:3). Why are we hidden? Well, the union that exists between Christ and His people is hidden from the eyes of the men and women of this world. Though they see us going about our daily tasks, they are unaware that our strength, by which we live and move and have our being, is drawn from God. That is why it is so

important to reach up to God daily for our strength—so that we will be able to act justly, love mercy, and walk humbly with our God (Micah 6:8).

What others see is the tip of the iceberg. They can't see what lies beneath the water line. Because we are hidden in Christ, we can find strength down deep—where others don't see.

ADDITIONAL NOTES

Read Colossians 3:1-4 in *The Message*.

> So if you're serious about living this new resurrection life with Christ, act like it. Pursue the things over which Christ presides. Don't shuffle along, eyes to the ground, absorbed with the things right in front of you. Look up, and be alert to what is going on around Christ—that's where the action is. See things from his perspective.
>
> Your old life is dead. Your new life, which is your real life—even though invisible to spectators—is with Christ in God. He is your life. When Christ (your real life, remember) shows up again on this earth, you'll show up, too—the real you, the glorious you. Meanwhile, be content with obscurity, like Christ.

How exciting to think that someday soon we will see the risen Christ in all His glory. When Christ returns, it will not just be His glory manifested. There will be glory for you and me expressed also, if we belong to Him.

GO DEEPER

Read the following verses. What do they say about your glory that will be revealed?

1 Corinthians 13:12

_____

_____

_____

Colossians 1:27

_____

_____

_____

1 John 3:2-3, 5

_____

_____

_____

Ladies, our Christian walk involves a process of becoming more like Him. This process will not be complete until we see Him face to face. Knowing this is our ultimate destiny should inspire us to purify ourselves and desire to reflect Him in our everyday lives.

Write 2 Timothy 2:21.

_____

_____

_____

What are you doing to keep yourself pure so that God can use you in the work He has planned for you?

_____

_____

_____

Close out today by reading Matthew 6:22-23. What does the "eye" refer to in this context?

_____

What do you think these verses mean?

_____

_____

_____

Our eyes are the pathway to our being. If they are good, we will see God clearly. But if our eyes are evil, they will shut out the light, clouding our view of God. A "pure" eye is one that is fixed on God.

I can remember a time in my life, after coming to a saving knowledge of Jesus Christ, when I was not walking in the light of God. One morning while I was driving, it felt like my spiritual eyes were replaced with worldly eyes. I don't know exactly how to explain it, except that my worldview took on a whole new vision—one not worthy of my calling. I was stunned by the experience and realized I was out of the will of God.

ADDITIONAL
NOTES

Do you find yourself in the same situation? If so, return to God. He will receive you with open arms. He desires for you to have a pure heart, clean hands, and clear eyes, so that your whole body will be full of light and have no darkness in it at all.

How fixed on God are you?

_____

_____

_____

Reflective prayer:
Write your thoughts, convictions, or insights.

_____

_____

_____

_____

_____

_____

[1] Walvoord and Zuck, The Bible Knowledge Commentary: New Testament, 680.

[2] Anders, Holman New Testament Commentary, 327

Day Two
A Transformed Lifestyle
is the Trademark of a New Life

Yesterday's lesson showed us that it is Christ who has changed our lives (Colossians 3:1-4); therefore, it is up to us to change our lifestyle.

Begin today by reading verses 5-11.

According to today's reading, how does change start? List the verse numbers.

_____

_____

What are the things we are urged to "take off," or put to death, according to verses 5-9?

_____

_____

_____

Paul tells us what things must be eliminated and gives us two reasons for their elimination: 1) we need to avoid the wrath of God, and 2) they reflect the way we once lived, but not anymore. Paul is calling for complete extermination, not careful management. He mentions three categories of behavior that must go: perverted passions, hot tempers, and sharp tongues.[1]

As we "take off" the old, it will take work on our part. The Bible never says that it would be easy. Let's take a look at how the New Testament portrays Christian living.

GO DEEPER

Read the following Scriptures and match each one with the person depicted.

1 Corinthians 9:24-27   Wrestler

2 Timothy 2:3-4   Athlete

2 Timothy 2:6   Farmer

Ephesians 6:12   Soldier

So, let us persevere as we move forward in God's power to live a lifestyle worthy of His calling.

You'll notice that the list of things we are exhorted to "take off" includes both external and internal areas. Some of the more obvious external areas (sexual immorality, lust, and evil desires) are ones we can physically see. But what about the ones that are more internal—the ones others don't always see, like greed?

In the Greek, "greed" *(pleonexia)*[2] means "a desire to have more." Greed of this sort seeks satisfaction in things below rather than in things above. Paul equates greed with idolatry.

Read Jeremiah 10:10-16 and answer the following questions regarding idol worship.

Who is the one true, living God?

_____

_____

What God will stand the test of time?

_____

_____

What mighty power and works do you see displayed in verses 12 and 13?

_____

_____

What do verses 14 and 15 tell us about idols?

_____

_____

What are some idols we make for ourselves?

_____

_____

ADDITIONAL NOTES

"HOLD EVERYTHING IN YOUR HANDS LIGHTLY; OTHERWISE, IT HURTS WHEN GOD PRIES THEM OUT."

—CORRIE TEN BOOM

The idols/gods we make for ourselves have no power in them. If we let the idols of money, fame, or power take the place of God, we deceive ourselves if we expect them to empower our lives.

Back up to Jeremiah 9:23-24. What are we *not* supposed to boast in?

_____

_____

Instead, what should we boast in?

_____

_____

Jeremiah warns us against boasting in our wisdom, might, and wealth. They may be valuable resources, but they should not be our ultimate priority. The only thing worth boasting about is our relationship with Jesus Christ. Wisdom, might, and wealth are merely means to an end.

John Maxwell, in his Leadership Bible,[3] recognizes the difference between worldly boasting and godly boasting with these two categories: The Ultimate and The Immediate:

The Ultimate	**The Immediate**
1. God is the source.	1. The others are a resource.
2. He provides a life.	2. These provide a living.
3. Spiritual things are the end.	3. Material things are a means.

Dear sister, what things are you holding on to so tightly that you are not willing to give up in order to let God be your ultimate priority?

_____

_____

_____

Write 1 Timothy 6:6-7.

_____

_____

_____

_____

What does 1 Timothy 6:6-7 mean to you personally?

_____

_____

_____

_____

So, now that you have "taken off" something, you will need to "put on" something. Paul uses the imagery of clothing. As believers, we are exhorted to discard our old, repulsive habits like a set of worn-out clothes. We are then urged to clothe ourselves with the kind of behaviors that will make us well dressed and appropriately fashionable. A transformed lifestyle should be the trademark of our new lives.

THE SECRET IS OUT

ADDITIONAL
NOTES

GO DEEPER

Look up the following Scriptures and share the added insights involved with "taking off" and "putting on" behaviors.

Ephesians 4:22-24

_____

_____

_____

Hebrews 12:1

_____

_____

_____

James 1:21

_____

_____

_____

Be aware that God may not change your circumstances or your situation. Instead, what God is really looking for is a heart change from you. I have heard Pastor Rick Warren say the reason for this is that "God is more interested in your character than your comfort; God is more interested in making your life holy than He is in making your life happy." God's Word should take up comfortable residence in your heart. Furthermore, all your activities and relationships should be viewed with spiritual significance. So, as you are continually being renewed, trust God with all your affairs.

Is there a circumstance in your life through which God is revealing Himself to you and changing you from the inside out?

_____

_____

_____

_____

Finish today with this little exercise of "taking off" and "putting on" from Colossians 3:12-13.

TOOK OFF

WILL PUT ON

Write in this shirt those habits or practices you have already "taken off" (put to death).

Write in this shirt what habits or practices you still need to "put on."

ADDITIONAL
NOTES

Reflective prayer:

Write your thoughts, convictions, or insights.

_____

_____

_____

_____

_____

_____

_____

_____

[1] Anders, Holman New Testament Commentary, 329.

[2] Ibid.

[3] John Maxwell Leadership Bible, second edition (Nashville: Maxwell Motivations, Inc, 2002, 2007), 920.

Day Three
Love is the Garment the World Sees; All Other Virtues are Undergarments

"Life," said one philosopher, "is a decision." We can decide to be angry or not to be angry, to lie or not to lie, to use offensive language or not to use it. It is foolish to believe that these things just flow out of us on their own accord. Before angry or inappropriate words come from our mouths, we have a moment of choice—to stop them or speak them. The moment of choice may be only a second—even a split second—but it is there, nevertheless.[1]

If our lives are under the rule of Christ as we read about in Colossians 3:7-10, then it follows that our decisions will come under His rule as well. So, it is just a question of willpower. You have to decide, "I will no longer do this."

In other words, you supply the willingness, and He will supply the power.

ADDITIONAL
NOTES

Read Colossians 3:12-15 for your strategy to live for Christ day by day.

How does Paul refer to his readers in verse 12?

_____

Can you confidently include yourself as one of the chosen and holy? (If not, please speak with your facilitator on how to know you are a child of God.)

_____

If so, what should you willfully clothe yourself with?

_____

_____

_____

According to verse 14, what is the most important thing to put on? Why?

_____

_____

_____

"Love," it has been said, "is a color that can be worn with anything—overalls or an evening dress." Or, you can think of it as a kind of overcoat, a garment that covers all other virtues. It brings harmony to all other disharmonies. Love is the garment the world sees. All other virtues are undergarments.[2]

How well are you loving others?

_____

_____

_____

Is there an article of clothing that is torn? List the steps you will take this week to begin to mend it.

_____

_____

_____

_____

Dear sister, there is only one way we can live out this renewed life for Christ. **What are we instructed to do in Colossians 3:16?**

_____

_____

In the Greek, "dwell" *(enoikeo)*[3] refers to "having a permanent residence; being at home." In the Message Bible, Eugene Peterson paraphrases it like this: "Let the word of Christ have the run of the house. Give it plenty of room in your lives."

When I was a young believer at the age of 18, I didn't read my Bible consistently for the first five years of my walk with God. But then I realized how much I wanted Christ to be at home in my heart. The only way I knew how to do that was to join a Bible study and develop an intimate relationship with Jesus. If this is your first Bible study, praise the Lord! Stay with it!

ADDITIONAL
NOTES

After joining the Bible study, I began to be enlightened by the Word of God, so I continued to seek out other studies. Many years into my studies, something changed: I started to desire the Word of God. It wasn't something I had to do, but rather it was something I wanted to do. Allowing the Word of God to dwell in me transformed my thinking and actions. In other words, He began to have the run of my house. I still have a long way to go, but this desire hasn't ceased. Ladies, the more we get to know Him, the more we will want to be like Him.

Have you allowed the Word of Christ to dwell in you? If yes, share how it has made a difference in your life.

_____

_____

_____

_____

If no, what do you need to do differently?

_____

_____

_____

GO DEEPER

Read the following Scriptures and write what each verse reveals to you about the Word of God.

Psalm 119:9

_____

Psalm 119:28

_____

Psalm 119:37

_____

Psalm 119:66

_____

Psalm 119:98

_____

Psalm 119:130

_____

If you're really feeling adventurous, read all of Psalm 119 and mark the impact the Word will have on your life.

Ephesians 5:26

_____

_____

2 Timothy 3:16

_____

_____

God's Word will have such a profound impact on our lives if we will just allow it to penetrate our hearts. The Word should dwell so much within us that we are rich with it. Just as a millionaire is rich with money, a Christian should also be rich with the Word.

ADDITIONAL
NOTES

Throughout all of the Scriptures, we read about men of God—Abraham, Moses, David, Daniel, Jeremiah, Peter, Paul, John and many others—who lived by the Word of God, hid the Word of God in their hearts, and meditated on the Word of God day and night.

 Read Joshua 1:8-9. What made Joshua so successful and prosperous?

_____

_____

_____

The success of Joshua's mission would lie in his personal obedience to the law of God. Our success also lies with our obedience to God and desire to meditate on His Word.

So, get into the Word of God and watch it make a difference in your daily life.

Ponder these questions as you close your time with the Lord today.

- How much time do you spend reading, studying, memorizing, and meditating on God's Word?

- Does the Word dwell in you abundantly, so much that you overflow with thankfulness in your heart to God?

- Do you share the wisdom from God's Word with others?

- Will you share what you are learning with someone this week?

Write a prayer committing yourself to the meditation of God's Word.

_____

_____

_____

_____

_____

Reflective prayer:

Write your thoughts, convictions, or insights.

_____

_____

_____

_____

_____

_____

_____

_____

[1] Selwyn Hughes, "Every Day with Jesus," Complete in Christ, March/ April 2008 (UK: CWR, 2008).

[2] Ibid.

[3] Strong, The New Strong's Exhaustive Concordance of the Bible.

Day Four
A Word to Wives

Before moving on to our relationships within our homes, let's read Colossians 3:17.

And whatever you do, whether in word or deed, do it all in the name of the Lord Jesus, giving thanks to God the Father through him.

Write what this verse says to you.

_____

_____

Dear sister, we are exhorted to do EVERYTHING as a representation of Him; in fact, Paul tells us to do it in His name, in His stead, and in His Spirit. Someone once put it this way: "We are the only Bible some people may read." This does not mean that we live our lives in fear that we may say or do something that misrepresents Christ. We are not supposed to be controlled by a spirit of fear, but by a spirit of thankfulness. We may never write a book, but by living for God we will be one! We will be open books, "epistles of Christ" for all to read.

ℰ

**WIFELY
SUBMISSION
IS THE DIVINE
CALLING TO
HONOR AND
AFFIRM HER
HUSBAND'S
LEADERSHIP AND
HELP CARRY
IT THROUGH
ACCORDING TO
HER GIFTS.[1]**

—JOHN PIPER

Read Ephesians 6:5-9. What do these verses reveal about how we can be like Christ on a daily basis?

_____

_____

_____

Wow! We should long to represent our Father just as Christ represents God. When we realize that our actions should represent our heavenly Father, it will make us stop and think about what our motives should be.

As we head into our study of the relationships within the family, may we remember that we are supposed to be representatives of Jesus Christ. Although Paul may be brief in his discussion on the Christian principles involved with the family, he certainly gets to the point.

Read Colossians 3:18-20. Identify the action verb Paul uses to show how each member of the family should behave. (I'll help you with the first one.)

Wife ____*Submit*____ Husband _____ Children _____

Okay ladies, we are going to camp on Colossians 3:18 for the remainder of today. But before you want to throw something at me or skip over this section, let's see what submission really means. Although my thoughts will be primarily directed to married women, I believe this subject is pertinent to those who are single as well. The Scriptures deal with the topic of submission in other relationships besides marriage—to employers (1 Peter 2:18), pastors (Hebrews 13:17), and civil government (Romans 13:1-7). Submission may take a different form in these relationships, but many of the principles still hold true.

First, how do you view submission?

_____

_____

_____

In this context, submit refers to a call to recognize and respond to the God-ordained authority of the husband or another authoritative person. Thus, God calls for submission between equals. If we are married women, we are not supposed to submit to all men, but rather to our own husbands. Conversely, we should not seek leadership from other men apart from our husbands, no matter how worthy they are of honor or respect. We must rather be subject to our own husbands.[2]

Let's begin by looking at Christ Himself. Christ is the model for equality with God and submission to the One to whom He is equal. Jesus Christ, although equal with God the Father, submitted to Him to carry out the plan for salvation. Likewise, although she is equal to man under God (Genesis 1:27), the wife should submit to her husband for the sake of their marriage and family. Submission involves mutual commitment and cooperation.

GO DEEPER

Read the following Scriptures and write what each one depicts about Christ in relation to His Father.

1 Corinthians 11:3

_____

_____

_____

1 Corinthians 15:28

_____

_____

_____

Now read Ephesians 5:21-24 and describe the relationship between our husbands and Christ.

_____

_____

_____

In her book _Feminine Appeal,_ Carolyn Mahaney says, "God reveals His ultimate intention for submission in marriage: It is to reflect the relationship between Christ and his church. The husband is to mirror the sacrificial love of Christ by laying down his life for his wife, and the wife is to exemplify the church's joyful submission to Christ by following her husband's leadership."[3]

Read 1 Peter 3:1-6. What truth is shared in verse 1?

_____

_____

_____

Of course, there are moral limits to this submission: it is [only] fitting in the Lord (Colossians 3:18). A wife's submission to her husband is only "in the Lord." That is, she is not obligated to follow her husband's leadership if it conflicts with scriptural commands or dishonors God in any way. A wife must never follow her husband's leadership into sin. Our preeminent authority is God Himself.

So, dear sister, before you and I can submit to our husbands, we must first submit to God. Without submission to God, submission to one's husband does not constitute a spiritual exercise.

A good question to ask yourself is this: "How can I help my husband today? What will make my husband's day better?" Is there something you have wanted to do for your husband, but you just haven't gotten around to it? Well, today is that day! Go for it and see what your husband's response is.

Look up the following practical ways to love your husband and match them with the correct action.[4]

Proverbs 12:25	Physically love him
Proverbs 21:5	Plan for him daily
Proverbs 31:15	Prepare for him daily
Romans 12:10	Respect him
1 Corinthians 7:3-5	Praise/encourage him
Ephesians 5:33	Honor him
Titus 2:4	Pray for him daily
James 5:16	Show love to him

Wow! After doing this exercise, how many of these actions do you practice on a daily basis? A weekly basis? Or on any basis? I believe that if we begin to practice these truths, we would begin to see a difference in our relationships with our husbands. Subsequently, this transformation would extend to our families and relationships outside our homes.

ADDITIONAL NOTES

In closing, I want to share with you a story from my own life regarding obedient submission.

We had lived in our first home for twelve years, and I loved my neighborhood. We raised our two daughters through elementary school, our neighbors nursed our family through my illness, and bonds of friendships were made. But due to some changes in the township, outside our backyard the residents voted to build a major grocery store there. So, my husband, John, decided it was time to look for a new home. The house-hunting process happened very fast, but with each day my desire to move began to wane. I certainly agreed that I didn't want our backyard to change, but I also didn't want my neighbors to change. Within three months, we sold our home and began to build another.

For many years prior to this move, I had felt God calling me to begin a neighborhood Bible study, which never came to fruition for one reason or another—or maybe just out of pure fear, I don't know. But I said to God, "If we make this move, I will begin the Bible study in our new neighborhood!"

So, after being obedient to my husband with the move, I now needed to be obedient to my God. For the first six months we lived in our new neighborhood, I walked our neighborhood and prayed for the eighty-plus homes and began to build relationships with the women. That fall, I sent out invitations to all the women and the neighborhood Bible study began with five. Through the years, it grew to over twenty women whose lives were changed by a relationship they formed with Jesus Christ. Praise the Lord!

So, out of submission to my husband and to my God, I was blessed beyond what I could have ever imagined or dreamed.

Share a "submission" story of your own with your group.

_____

_____

_____

_____

_____

Reflective prayer:

Write your thoughts, convictions, or insights.

_____

_____

_____

_____

_____

_____

_____

ADDITIONAL
NOTES

[1] John Piper and Wayne Grudem, Recovering Biblical Manhood and Womanhood (Wheaton, Illinois: Crossway Books, 2006), 53.

[2] Carolyn Mahaney, Feminine Appeal (Wheaton, IL: Crossway Books, 2003), 125.

[3] Mahaney, Feminine Appeal, 122.

[4] Elizabeth George, A Woman After God's Own Heart: Bible Study Workbook (Dallas: The Sampson Company, 2004), 64.

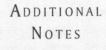

Day Five
Family Ties

Let's refresh our memory on the husband's role, according to Colossians 3:19.

Read the following verses. For each, discuss how husbands should relate to their wives.

Colossians 3:19

_____

_____

_____

Ephesians 5:25-33

_____

_____

_____

1 Peter 3:7

_____

_____

_____

Husbands are supposed to exercise loving leadership, not dictatorial dominion. Both men and women need these reminders that we have looked at over the past two days. Men need the reminder to be tender and loving as much as women need to remember not to take the rightful place of their husbands' God-given authority. So, in a maturing marriage, the husband exercises compassionate care, and his wife responds by willingly submitting to his loving leadership.

What does 1 Peter 3:7 say will be hindered if the husband does not treat his wife lovingly?

_____

_____

_____

A living relationship with God depends on right relationships with others. If men use their position to mistreat their wives, their prayers will not be heard. This principle not only holds true for family relationships, but also carries over to all relationships.

Read Matthew 5:23-24. What are you supposed to do if you have a grievance with someone?

_____

_____

_____

Now, on to the role of the children. Obviously, Paul's principles are for children who have reached the age of understanding. He tells them that they also must come under the rule of Christ.

GO DEEPER

Read the following verses. Identify the principle for children mentioned in each one.

Colossians 3:20

_____

_____

_____

Exodus 20:12

_____

_____

_____

Proverbs 6:20-23

_____

_____

_____

Ephesians 6:1-3

_____

_____

_____

Disobedience to parents in the Old Testament was called rebellion against God and was severely punished (Exodus 21:17, Leviticus 20:9). Jesus set an example for all children by obeying His parents, Joseph and Mary, when He returned to Nazareth with them after they found Him speaking with the religious leaders in the temple (Luke 2:51).

Obedience reflects God's design for order in the family. The fifth commandment in Exodus 20:12 is the only commandment that contains a promise: "that it may be well with you and you may live a long life on the earth."

Once I remember listening to a sermon on children obeying and respecting their parents and thinking, Wow, I wish my girls were here to listen to this one. By the end of the service, however, I realized that it wasn't only for children being reared, but also for me as a grown child. Adult children also have a responsibility to the Lord: to respect their parents as they age. Obedience may take on another form as we mature, but respect never loses its grip.

It is a blessing when our children obey us and heed our advice, isn't it? Additionally, as parents, we play an important role in the family dynamics.

Read Colossians 3:21, Proverbs 1:8, and 6:20.

Who do these Scriptures address?

_____

_____

_____

_____

Only fathers are mentioned in Colossians 3:21 because they are the head of the house, but you can clearly see that the same principle applies to mothers as well, according to the verses from Proverbs.

How does Ephesians 6:4, along with Colossians 3:21, say fathers should care for their children?

_____

_____

_____

If you are a parent doing this study, you are not supposed to frustrate your children, because it will just stir up evil emotions within them. This will discourage their love for the Lord. Praise for well-doing rather than constant criticism, along with loving discipline, will help you rear your children in the training and instruction of the Lord (Ephesians 6:4).

Okay, if you are like me, you have royally messed this one up at times. So, what do you do about it? Begin again! Ask God to give you strength and wisdom. Watch for ways to praise and encourage your children.

In what ways do your family relationships need to change to make them pleasing unto the Lord?

_____

_____

_____

If you are not married or may not have experienced parenting yet, thank you for staying with us through these two days.

ADDITIONAL
NOTES

I know that, for myself, I have been extremely thankful for those "spiritual moms" who have not only poured into my individual life, but also have been deeply involved in my girls' lives as we have raised them. It is vital for your children to have other adults and friends who can pour godly advice into their lives. Let's face it. At times they may not want to listen to us, but if the same advice comes from someone else, they may be inclined to listen.

Reflective prayer:
Write your thoughts, convictions, or insights.

_____

_____

_____

_____

_____

_____

_____

Week Three
Video Session

_____

_____

_____

_____

_____

_____

_____

_____

_____

_____

_____

_____

_____

_____

_____

_____

_____

_____

Colossians
Week Four

Day One
Relationships in the Workplace

Day Two
First, Talk with God

Day Three
**Faithfulness, Faithfulness
is What I Want from You**

Day Four
**Meanings Behind the Name
(Part 1)**

Day Five
**Meanings Behind the Name
(Part 2)**

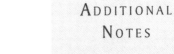

Day One
Relationships in the Workplace

As we finish up our study of Colossians 3, we'll look at our responsibilities to others, our work ethic, relationships in the workplace, and those in authority.

Read Colossians 3:22-25, along with 1 Timothy 6:1-2 and 1 Peter 2:18-25.

What words might be substituted today for servants and masters?

_____

_____

When is God pleased with you (1 Peter 2:18-25)?

_____

_____

KNOWING THE
TRUTH ABOUT
CHRISTIAN
LIVING INVITES
US TO LIVE
AN ORDINARY
LIFE IN AN
EXTRAORDINARY
WAY.

—MAX ANDERS

For whom should you do your work? Why?

_____

_____

_____

In what manner are you supposed to perform your work?

_____

_____

As Christian employees, we should do the job that is expected of us—and not just when the boss is watching. We have a Master in heaven who observes both our internal attitude and external performance.[1] Our paycheck may come from our employer, but our true reward is from the Lord.

Read Proverbs 6:6-11. What do you learn from the ant?

_____

_____

_____

Apparently, ants have no leader—no commander to direct them, no overseer to inspect their work, no ruler to encourage them. Yet they work better than some people with a leader! What about you? Do you produce good work only when someone is watching? Or, do you recognize that since all your service is for God, you do your best at all times—even when no human authority is watching? Ladies, no matter who your boss is, you are really working for God.

Share about an occasion when you put your whole heart into your work, doing it unto the Lord rather than for other people. How was it evident?

_____

_____

_____

In Colossians 3:25 (NLT), Paul tells us, "Those who do wrong will be paid back for the wrong they have done. God has no favorites who can get away with evil." How many times are you apt to take matters into your own hands, instead of allowing God to avenge you? This verse clearly states that God will take care of those who do evil—if not in this life, the one to come.

Read Colossians 4:1. What does it say masters (those in authority) are supposed to do? Why?

_____

_____

_____

Paul begins chapter 3 by urging believers to "look above." He closes the chapter in the same way. The apostle exhorts wives to "look above" to Christ as their example of submission. Similarly, he encourages husbands to "look above" to Christ as their example of love. He admonishes children to "look above" to Christ as their example of obedience. Moreover, Paul inspires slaves to "look above" to Christ as their impartial rewarder. Finally, he reminds masters to "look above" to Christ as their heavenly judge.[2]

ADDITIONAL NOTES

MY DEAR BROTHERS AND SISTERS, TAKE NOTE OF THIS: EVERYONE SHOULD BE QUICK TO LISTEN, SLOW TO SPEAK AND SLOW TO BECOME ANGRY, BECAUSE HUMAN ANGER DOES NOT PRODUCE THE RIGHTEOUSNESS THAT GOD DESIRES.

—JAMES 1:19-20

In these kinds of relationships, are there changes that need to take place in your life as far as seeking and/or serving the Lord?

_____

_____

_____

As I studied Colossians 4:1, it came to my attention that the strong link between master and slave discussed by Paul was largely due to the unique situation in Colossae, where the runaway slave, Onesimus, was returning to his master, Philemon.

I think it's worth going down a bunny trail to look at the short Book of Philemon. Philemon lived in Colossae, and the church met in his house.

Look ahead to Colossians 4:9. Who accompanied Tychicus on the journey to Colossae?

_____

_____

_____

Read Philemon 1-25 for a beautiful reminder of our responsibility to Christian brotherhood. Answer the following questions and cite the verses that apply.

What was Paul's relationship to Philemon?

_____

_____

What did Paul want Philemon to do? Why?

_____

_____

Why did Paul not order Philemon to do what he actually wanted him to do?

_____

_____

What transpired in Onesimus's life since he last saw Philemon?

_____

_____

What did Paul offer to do for Onesimus? Why?

_____

_____

_____

How does what Paul was willing to do for Onesimus relate to what Christ has done for us?

_____

_____

_____

Is there someone you need to forgive, as Philemon needed to forgive Onesimus?

_____

ADDITIONAL
NOTES

Reflective prayer:

Write your thoughts, convictions, or insights.

_____

_____

_____

_____

_____

_____

_____

[1] Anders, Holman New Testament Commentary, 333.
[2] Ibid, 334.

Day Two
First, Talk with God

Paul gives some final instruction on Christian conduct in Colossians 4. Let's see where we should begin as we walk in a manner worthy of the Lord.

How important is prayer in your life? Doesn't it seem like your prayer life is always an area you want to improve? I know that for me it is. Paul points out in Colossians 4:2 that before we talk to others about God, we ought to talk to God about others.

Read Colossians 4:2 and list the three things that should accompany prayer.

_____

_____

Prayer should be done with diligence. "Devote" means "to be busily engaged in; persist in; or give constant attention to." In our lives, prayer should not just be an option for occasional emergencies. If we are going to withstand the constant pressures of this world, we must adopt an attitude of persistent prayer.[1]

ADDITIONAL NOTES

Is there an area in your life that you need constant prayer in?

_____

_____

Is there an area that you have given up praying about? Why?

_____

_____

_____

Our faith shouldn't die if the answers don't come quick enough, for the delay may be God's way of working out His will in our lives. When you get tired of praying, know that God is always present, always listening, always answering—maybe not in the way you had hoped for, but in ways that He knows is best.

Look up Isaiah 55:8-9. Describe God's ways and thoughts.

_____

_____

_____

This insight on being alert in your prayer life from C. S. Lewis can be helpful:

No one in his senses, if he has any power of ordering his own day, would reserve his chief prayers for bedtime—obviously the worst possible hour for any action which needs concentration. . . . My own plan, when hard pressed, is to seize any time, and place, however unsuitable, in preference to the last waking moment. . . . The body ought to pray as well as the head.[2]

What does Matthew 6:1-15 say regarding prayer?

_____

_____

_____

_____

In Matthew's day, some people, especially the religious leaders, wanted to be seen as "holy." Public prayer was one way to get that kind of attention. Jesus saw through their self-righteousness and taught that the essence of prayer is not public but private communication with God. Yes, there is a time for public prayer in a believer's life, but to only pray when others will notice indicates that the real audience is not God, but man. We continually need to assess our motives regarding what we do for God.

Continue reading Colossians 4:2-4 and answer the following questions:

For whom in particular does Paul request prayer?

_____

What is his specific prayer?

_____

_____

How did Paul want to proclaim it?

_____

_____

I often find it amazing that Paul didn't ask for prayer to relieve his situation of imprisonment. He did not pray with selfish gain in mind. Instead, he prayed that God would open a door of opportunity to share God's secret plan of Jesus with others. I am going to be honest here. I am not sure that would have been my first request. Yet Paul knew God was able to open doors even for those behind prison doors.

 Even though you're not in prison, you may be in a situation or time in your life when you aren't seeing doors open. Would you like to share this with your group so they can pray for you?

_____

_____

_____

 Or, you may have had the opportunity to share with someone and want to encourage your group. Share that, too.

_____

_____

_____

Paul will now shift his evangelistic interests from himself to the believers at Colossae. He shares how believers should treat "outsiders" or unbelievers. We must be wise in the way we act toward outsiders. Wisdom enables us to combine boldness with tact. If we desire to be effective, we must make the most of every opportunity.

Read Colossians 4:5-6. What do you believe "make the most of every opportunity" is referring to?

_____

_____

_____

Using Colossians 4:6, answer the following questions:

What should our conversation be full of?

_____

What should it be seasoned with?

_____

What purpose should our conversation serve?

_____

Dear sister, for the message of Christ to be effective, our walk must be accompanied by flavorful talk. **What do you think that might look like?**

_____

_____

_____

Salt was used for two purposes in Paul's time. It was used both as a preservative to keep food from spoiling and an additive to flavor food. So, what does that look like for us today in the twenty-first century? It means our speech should be free from corruption and wholesome, as well as interesting and appealing.[3] The art of seasoning our speech with just enough salt should be done so that our conversation won't be so saturated that it drives "outsiders" away.

"FOR ATTRACTIVE LIPS, SPEAK WORDS OF KINDNESS.

FOR LOVELY EYES, SEEK OUT THE GOOD IN PEOPLE.

FOR A SLIM FIGURE, SHARE YOUR FOOD WITH THE HUNGRY.

FOR BEAUTIFUL HAIR, LET A CHILD RUN THEIR FINGERS THROUGH IT ONCE A DAY.

FOR POISE, WALK WITH THE KNOWLEDGE THAT YOU NEVER WALK ALONE."

—AUDREY HEPBURN

Imagine you are getting out the ingredients to cook a batch of cookies, but you have unknowingly mixed up the salt and sugar. You end up putting in a dash of sugar and a cup of salt. Now picture a little boy taking a big bite of one of those cookies. How long will it take the child to realize something is wrong? Do you think he will ask for another cookie? Of course not!

The art of seasoning is a matter of balance. Just enough salt to notice, but not too much to overwhelm. Salt creates a thirst, a desire for water. A desire for more.

As Christians, we sprinkle the salt of God's grace and gospel into our daily conversation. We don't saturate every conversation in a way that drives others away. The artful seasoning of God's loving grace into our conversation will create a thirst, a desire in the lives of others. They will long to know more of Jesus.[4]

 What does Ephesians 4:29 and 5:4 say about gracious speech?

_____

_____

_____

What, if anything, do you need to do to make your talk more gracious?

_____

_____

_____

Reflective prayer:

Write your thoughts, convictions, or insights.

_____

_____

_____

_____

_____

_____

_____

[1] Anders, Holman New Testament Commentary.

[2] C. S. Lewis, The Joyful Christian (New York: Macmillan Publishing Co., 1977) 88-89.

[3] Anders, Holman New Testament Commentary.

[4] NIV Women of Faith Study Bible (Grand Rapids, MI: Zondervan, 2001).

Day Three
Faithfulness, Faithfulness is What I Want from You

With so many churches close to Paul's heart, how was he able to keep up with each one? He wasn't Superman. Thankfully, Paul had help.

In the ending verses of his epistle to the Colossians, Paul does more than just offer a personal sign-off. He also gives us a glimpse into his friendships and fellowship of encouragement. The people we will study are real, ordinary individuals who helped Paul carry out an extraordinary task for the sake of an extraordinary Savior.

Read Colossians 4:7-9, along with Ephesians 6:21. List the people Paul mentions and describe their character.

_____

_____

_____

_____

_____

Tychicus was a faithful and beloved brother. He was also mentioned in Acts 20:4, Ephesians 6:21, and Titus 3:12 as one who accompanied Paul on portions of his third journey. As Tychicus was faithful with seemingly small things, such as encouraging the people at Ephesus (2 Timothy 4:12) and the people of Crete (Titus 3:12), he was blessed with greater things in his later years. Paul found him faithful.

Read the familiar Parable of the Talents recorded in Luke 19:11-27. What do you think is the main point of this parable?

_____

_____

_____

The Parable of the Talents stresses the need to serve the King while He is away. How are you serving Christ as you wait for His return? Are you using your talents (time, money, and abilities) for the glory of God?

What are the talents and gifts you are using for God?

_____

_____

_____

Let's continue to take a look at the spiritual gifts God gives to His people.

GO DEEPER

 Look up the following passages and list the spiritual gifts God has distributed to His people.

Romans 12:6-11

_____

_____

_____

1 Corinthians 12:7-11

_____

_____

_____

1 Peter 4:10-11

_____

_____

_____

According to 1 Corinthians 12:7, why are these gifts given to you?

_____

_____

Are you being faithful with the talents and gifts God has given you?

_____

ADDITIONAL NOTES

If not, what is hindering you?

_____

_____

_____

_____

The virtues you may have written down regarding Tychicus could have included "dear brother," "faithful minister," and "fellow-servant." The most significant thing about Tychicus was that he was "a faithful minister." Recognizing that he had a call on his life, Tychicus was faithful to that call, which gave him drive and direction. Nevertheless, he did not allow his single-mindedness to prevent him from being a dear brother and fellow-servant. [1]

At times, you and I may become extremely busy and absorbed in fulfilling our life mission. Or, we may be considered by our co-workers as faithful servants, but are we considered "dear sisters" or good "fella-servants"? Are there times that you are so caught up in your ministry activities that you cannot take care of others? We all should be like Tychicus, who was a well-rounded person, faithful in his ministry while still maintaining care and concern for others.

How well rounded are you? Explain.

_____

_____

_____

_____

Is there something God is calling you "out" of in order to make Him your priority and be more loving to those around you?

_____

_____

_____

Close out today by writing 1 John 4:11-12.

_____

_____

_____

Today, others will clearly see God by the way we love them. I pray that you will be a beacon to someone today through your faithfulness, love, and caring. Go and be that display of Christ to the person who needs to see the face of God today. Love you, dear sister!

Reflective prayer:
Write your thoughts, convictions, or insights.

_____

_____

_____

_____

[1] Selwyn Hughes, "Every Day with Jesus," Complete in Christ, March/ April 2008 (UK: CWR, 2008).

GO AND BE THAT DISPLAY OF CHRIST TO THE PERSON WHO NEEDS TO SEE THE FACE OF GOD TODAY.

Day Four
Meanings Behind the Name
(Part 1)

We will continue to look into the character and lives of Paul's companions today.

Read Colossians 4:10-13 and write down the names of the men mentioned.

_____

_____

_____

Go Deeper

Let's dig deeper into the Scriptures to find out more about these men.

Aristarchus – 4:10a

Paul refers to Aristarchus as a fellow prisoner. This could mean that he either attended to Paul while in prison, or he was confined to prison for the very same reason as the apostle—preaching the gospel.

Read Acts 19:29, 20:2-4, and 27:1-2. What is the added insight you've discovered about Aristarchus?

_____

_____

_____

Aristarchus was a devoted companion to Paul. He was always there when Paul needed him, whether the apostle was in prison, an Ephesian riot, or a shipwreck. Adversity did not lessen his affection for Paul. Now, that is some kind of friend.

What does Romans 5:3 say adversity will produce?

_____

_____

_____

Have you seen this chain reaction in your own life? If yes, share your experience.

_____

_____

_____

James tells us to consider it pure joy whenever we face trials of any kind (James 1:2). This can be hard at times when you are going through a difficult situation. When I look back at those afflictions in my own life, I am thankful for what God has brought me through and what He has taught me. If you are in the middle of an affliction today, please try to be the best learner you can in the situation. When you come through it by God's power, others will be drawn to Him because of your steadfastness.

Read 2 Corinthians 1:8-11 and answer the following questions.

Who did Paul rely on throughout this hardship?

_____

_____

_____

In verse 10, what did Paul say God did for him?

_____

_____

What activity on the part of other believers helped Paul with his deliverance (v. 11)?

_____

In the Greek, "deliver" *(rhuomai)*[1] means "to draw to oneself."

Dear sister, God may not always remove the obstacle in your life because He knows the details of your life, from the beginning to the end. He knows what it is going to take for you to become more like Him. What He will do for you through the trial is draw you unto Himself. If you make the Most High your shelter, no evil will conquer you because He orders His angels to protect you (Psalm 91:10-11). This is not to say that trials won't come, because you know they will. But they will not conquer you if you allow Him to rescue you.

Let's move on to Paul's next companion, John Mark (Colossians 4:10b).

ADDITIONAL NOTES

TRIALS WILL NOT CONQUER YOU IF YOU ALLOW HIM TO RESCUE YOU.

Read Acts 12:12; 13:5,13; 15:36-40; and 2 Timothy 4:11. Write down the added insights you glean regarding Mark.

_____

_____

_____

_____

_____

_____

John Mark is also the writer of the Gospel of Mark. He is not one of the original twelve disciples, but he accompanied Barnabas on Paul's first missionary journey. Although Mark did fail to stay with them on the entire trip and was not asked to accompany Paul on the second journey, he and Barnabas broke away from Paul to go on their own missionary journey. More than a dozen years later, Mark was reunited back with Paul (Philemon 24).

Re-read Acts 15:36-40. What did Paul and Barnabas's disagreement cause?

_____

_____

Do you see this as a good or bad thing? Why or why not?

_____

_____

This story shows us that God will even work through conflict and disagreement. Scholars agree that both Paul and Barnabas were right in their assessment of Mark. It may have been too soon for Mark to venture out with such a pro-Gentile apostle as Paul, but Barnabas certainly saw good, raw material in his cousin, Mark.[2]

Disagreement is not always a bad thing, as we see here. This disagreement caused two great men to reach more people separately than together. Mark's biography proves that one failure in life does not mean the end of usefulness. Oh thank you, Lord Jesus!

Is there something in your past that is keeping you from doing the work God has called you to?

_____

_____

_____

Is there someone you are holding back from working for the Lord? Is there someone you need to give a second chance to, like Paul did for Mark?

_____

_____

_____

Our next individual is Justus. Justus is an unknown colleague of Paul; in fact, Colossians 4:11 is the only place in the Scriptures where he is mentioned—that he brings comfort to Paul.

As we finish out the day, we will look at one more companion, Epaphras.

ADDITIONAL NOTES

ONE FAILURE IN LIFE DOES NOT MEAN THE END OF USEFULNESS.

Read Colossians 1:7, 4:12-13, and Philemon 23. List the added insights you find about Epaphras.

_____

_____

_____

_____

We met Epaphras in the opening days of this study. Paul has already told us several things about him. Now, he adds, "He is always wrestling in prayer for you." Epaphras was the man responsible for bringing the gospel to the Colossians. Epaphras went into battle, praying continually with purpose. Aware of what the Colossians were facing, he knew their immediate need was to grow to maturity in Christ in order to resist the false teaching taking place in Colossae. Not only did Epaphras pray earnestly for Colossae, but Laodicea and Hierapolis as well.

The phrase "wrestled in prayer" suggests that his prayers were largely intercessory.

Read Genesis 18:16-33 regarding Abraham's intercession with God over Sodom and answer the following questions.

What does Abraham's prayer teach you about intercession?

_____

_____

_____

What does it teach you about God?

_____

_____

_____

Dear sister, we can come to God asking anything, with the understanding that His answers will always come from His perspective. You may be missing God's answer to a prayer of yours because you may not have considered any possible answer other than the one you have been expecting.

Every church and ministry needs an Epaphras. Take a moment to thank God for the "Epaphrases" in your life.

_____

_____

_____

_____

_____

_____

_____

_____

ADDITIONAL
NOTES

Reflective prayer:

Write your thoughts, convictions, or insights.

_____

_____

_____

_____

_____

_____

_____

_____

[1] Strong, The New Strong's Exhaustive Concordance of the Bible.

[2] Walvoord and Zuck, The Bible Knowledge Commentary: New
    Testament.

Day Five
Meanings Behind the Name
(Part 2)

I hope you are enjoying as much as I am learning more about Paul's companions and how we can apply their character traits and virtues to our own lives. We will close out Week Four by continuing to learn from Paul's friends, Luke and Demas.

We will begin with Luke (Colossians 4:14a).

Read Colossians 4:14, Acts 16:10, 20:6, 21:15, and 2 Timothy 4:11. Write down the added insights you find regarding Luke.

_____

_____

_____

Definitely, one of Paul's most enduring companions was his dear friend, Luke, the talented specialist. Luke is the writer of the Gospel bearing his name (Luke 1:1) and the Book of Acts (Acts 1:1). If you were to study Acts, you would see that Luke accompanied Paul on portions of his second and third missionary journeys. He traveled with him to Jerusalem and then on to Rome by ship and stormy seas.

Luke, the doctor, was deeply appreciated by Paul and the others as they traveled because many times they found themselves greeted with whips and stones. Some say it is even possible that Paul's "thorn in the flesh" could have been some kind of physical ailment that needed Luke's constant attention (2 Corinthians 12:1-10). The Scriptures aren't clear on Paul's "thorn in the flesh," but this is an interesting observation, nonetheless.

Read Proverbs 17:17, John 3:27-29, and 15:12-13. Record what it says about true friendship.

_____

_____

_____

_____

I hope you have some friends like Luke—friends who are there for you to listen to you, help and encourage you, and sacrifice themselves for your well-being. I am grateful that God has blessed me with many women who are good friends like Luke was for Paul. Earlier in the study, I mentioned a time when I was hospitalized for four months. Well, during that hospital stay, I had many friends and family members who pitched in to help my husband, John. I would like to share with you about one in particular. This dear friend sacrificed herself and her life for mine. She brought everything she was involved with to a screeching halt to take care of my two girls, a toddler and infant, four days a week so that John would not have to put them in day care. She cared for my girls as if they were her very own.

Months later, after I recovered, I asked her why and how she did it. She responded, "I was doing it unto God, and the Holy Spirit gave me the strength I needed every day." The effect of this sacrificial act of kindness went far beyond our immediate family. It also touched the lives of all who knew her and is still touching those who hear about her self-sacrificing love for a friend. She was the greatest example of friendship to me, one whom I want to emulate. Okay, let me go grab a box of tissues now. . . .

Luke did not walk with Jesus here on this earth, so he did not have first-hand accounts. But, he was an avid historian. Because the truth was so important to Luke, he relied heavily on eyewitness accounts. Just as it was important for Luke to "check out" his sources, it is important for us as well.

Refresh your memory by reading Acts 17:10-12. What does it say the Bereans did?

_____

_____

We will finish up with the last of Paul's companions, Demas (Colossians 4:14b).

Read Colossians 4:14, along with 2 Timothy 4:10, for a look into the life of Demas. What is known about Demas?

_____

_____

_____

ADDITIONAL
NOTES

Yes, Demas was still at Paul's side when Paul wrote Colossians. Yet, at the end of Paul's life, Demas fell in love with the world and forsook Paul.

GO DEEPER

Take a moment and contrast Demas and Luke in your own words.

_____

_____

_____

Look up the following Scriptures and write what each one says regarding the things of this world.

1 Corinthians 7:31

_____

_____

_____

2 Corinthians 4:17-18

_____

_____

_____

James 4:4

_____

_____

_____

1 John 2:15-17

_____

_____

_____

How do these Scriptures speak to you personally?

_____

_____

_____

Wow! Knowing that this evil world and our desires for its pleasures will end one day can help give us courage to control our greed and self-indulgence so that we will continue to do God's will.

As we close these last two days, let's recap the traits of these companions of Paul. Match the person with the virtue.

Aristarchus   Forgiven, reunited

Mark   Devoted

Epaphras   Compassionate

Luke   Prayer warrior

Demas   Worldly

ADDITIONAL
NOTES

Which one of these men do you most closely relate with and why?

_____

_____

_____

Reflective prayer:

Write your thoughts, convictions, or insights.

_____

_____

_____

_____

_____

_____

_____

Week Four
Video Session

Colossians
Week Five

Day One
House Churches

Day Two
Learn it. Live it. Pass it On.

Day Three
An Encouraging Word

Day Four
Closing Words

Day Five
Grace be unto You

Day One
House Churches

Week Five will bring our journey through Colossians to a close. It may be a short book, but there is a lot packed into the four chapters. I hope you have been encouraged to keep Christ, the visible image of the invisible God, preeminent in your life. We will finish with Paul's challenges to his beloved churches.

Paul not only sent a letter to Colossae, but also to Laodicea. We don't know much about the letter to Laodicea, except that it was important and Paul wanted it read aloud to the Colossians.

Read Colossians 4:15. Who were the Colossians supposed to greet?

_____

_____

_____

ADDITIONAL
NOTES

During the first and second century, the church met in individual homes. Considered house churches, they were quite common in the New Testament times.

GO DEEPER

Read the following Scriptures. In addition to the church that met in Nympha's home, list the church houses and where they met.

Acts 12:12

_____

Acts 16:12-15, 40

_____

Acts 18:7

_____

Romans 16:3-5 and 1 Corinthians 16:19

_____

Philemon 1-2

_____

For the most part, the early church met for worship, prayer, instruction, and fellowship in homes. Today there is a rise of house churches emerging alongside traditional churches. It shouldn't matter if we attend a traditional church or we're part of a small community house church. Our homes should be used to encourage and welcome others.

Read Titus 2:3-5. Discuss Paul's exhortations for the older women to teach the younger women.

_____

_____

_____

You may be thinking to yourself, I don't host a church in my home. But then again, you may be a woman who does host a church in her home. Either way, it is vital in the lives of those who enter your home that you develop a heart for your home.

Read Proverbs 14:1 and complete the following statements based on this Scripture:

A wise woman

_____

_____

A foolish woman

_____

_____

What are some areas in women's lives that tear down or destroy their homes?

_____

_____

_____

Read Proverbs 24:3-4. List the three things needed to build, establish, and furnish a home.

_____

_____

_____

I am so thankful that the Lord gives us the wisdom from above. Indeed, from His mouth comes knowledge and understanding (Proverbs 2:6).

Dear sister, we don't have to walk this journey alone. We have a Savior who wants to help us build our homes by pouring His life into them, making them a place of worship.

As we "build" our homes, we will need to be diligent about our work. Read the following Scriptures and then write down the insights that encourage you to stay the course and be more diligent.

Psalm 39:4-5

_____

_____

_____

Psalm 90:12

_____

_____

_____

Ephesians 2:10

_____

_____

_____

Ephesians 5:15-16

_____

_____

_____

1 Timothy 5:14

_____

_____

_____

ADDITIONAL NOTES

The command in Titus 2 to be "working at home" is further illustrated in 1 Timothy 5:14. Paul says, "So I counsel younger widows to marry, to have children, to manage their homes and to give the enemy no opportunity for slander." In the Greek, "manage their homes" literally means "to be the ruler, despot, or master of the home."[1] So, ladies, we see that this is not a role we can take lightly. We are exhorted to function as the home manager by taking full responsibility for the domestic duties of the household. The Scriptures are clear on this subject. For a married couple, the man is responsible for providing for the household (1 Timothy 5:8), while the woman is supposed to be the caretaker of the household.

Now, the Bible does not say that women cannot work outside of the home, nor does it discourage them from receiving wages for work.

ADDITIONAL
NOTES

The Scriptures provide many examples of women who worked in other settings and earned income, but never neglected their families and homes.

I can remember a time in my marriage when our girls were in elementary school. I was working through a Bible study that encouraged us to ask our spouses, according to the Titus 2 mandate, what we could be doing better. Well, I knew that I didn't even need to ask my husband because just the week before, he asked me to do something for him in the house, and I didn't complete it for a few days. He then continued to say to me, "If so and so asked you to do it or the school needed it done, it would have been done yesterday." Ouch! Right then, I knew I wasn't taking care of my home the way God intended for me to. To accomplish this goal, I needed to make my home a priority in the life of my family and diligently watch over the affairs of my home (Proverbs 31:27).

Is there something you have been putting off doing in your home because you are just too busy to attend to the matter at hand? Begin by managing your schedule better to allow time for your home.

FOLLOW HIM,
SHARE HIM,
AND
GLORIFY HIM.

Take a moment and think about your day/week. Write down what transpires in your home, from taking care of little ones to meetings that take place in your home.

_____

_____

_____

_____

_____

Are you using your home as a place to encourage and minister to others?

_____

If no, why not?

_____

_____

_____

Pray for ways that God can use you and your home to represent the gospel.

Finish today by reading Proverbs 31:10-31. List the areas this noble woman tends to, both outside and within the home.

_____

_____

_____

_____

_____

Even though this capable woman pursued many endeavors beyond her home, her primary motive and goal was to serve her family and her home. Whether we're single, married, working outside the home, or stay-at-home moms, our goal should be the same: working at home should always remain an ongoing priority in our lives.

ADDITIONAL
NOTES

Reflective prayer:

Write your thoughts, convictions, or insights.

_____

_____

_____

_____

_____

_____

_____

_____

_____

_____

[1] Mahaney, Feminine Appeal, 94.

Day Two
Learn it. Live it. Pass it on.

As we begin to close out this study, I am convicted by the final words penned by Paul from Colossians 4:16-17 (NLT).

> After you have read this letter, pass it on to the church at Laodicea so they can read it, too. And you should read the letter I wrote to them. And say to Archippus, "Be sure to carry out the ministry the Lord gave you."

 What two things from Colossians 4:16-17 are we exhorted to do?

1. _____

2. _____

Dear ones, God wants you to share what we've studied—the wisdom we've gained and the truth that has transformed our lives. So, as we've worked through this letter from Paul, you have learned from it. You have been encouraged to live it out and pass it on. Be sure that you're diligent to what God has called you to!

ADDITIONAL NOTES

It can be a little scary at times to share God's Word with others. After hearing God's call to share His Word with women at a conference I attended in 1996, God opened that door in my new neighborhood two years later, with much uncertainty on my part. I had no idea what it would become or where God would take it. Many years have passed, and multitudes of women have been reached, not only through the neighborhood Bible study, but an interdenominational Bible study as well. All this has occurred through my obedience to share His letters with women. If God can use me, an ordinary stay-at-home mom, He can use YOU! Be diligent and passionate about what God has called you to do. Learn it, live it, and pass it on. . . .

Read Ezekiel 3:1-5. What is the instruction given to Ezekiel?

_____

_____

_____

_____

How important is it for you to digest the Word of God before moving out?

_____ Vital   _____ Somewhat important   _____ Not important

Is there something God is calling you to do? Do you feel Him tugging on your heartstrings to pass something on to that person you have been reluctant to talk with?

Dear sister, time is fleeting! Now is the time.

Read Jeremiah 1:6-9 and answer the following questions:

What was Jeremiah's excuse?

_____

What was the Lord's reply?

_____

_____

_____

Who should you not be afraid of?

_____

Why are you not supposed to be afraid?

_____

Now read Jeremiah 1:17-19. What added insight from this passage encourages you?

_____

_____

_____

If you have a list of excuses longer than Pinocchio's nose and have not carried out what God is calling you to do, maybe that is all they are . . . excuses. Please take time to sit with the Lord and talk with Him to see if now is the time to carry out His plan. For such a time is this to make a difference in your family, your home, your community, and your church.

ADDITIONAL NOTES

FOR SUCH A TIME AS THIS TO MAKE A DIFFERENCE IN YOUR FAMILY, YOUR HOME, YOUR COMMUNITY, AND YOUR CHURCH.

ADDITIONAL
NOTES

 Read Nehemiah 6:8-11 and answer the following questions:

What did Nehemiah's enemies want to see happen?

_____

_____

_____

How did Nehemiah respond?

_____

_____

_____

Ladies, don't allow the Enemy to divert or stop you from doing the task God has called you to. Sometimes the pressure is too great, and our first reaction may be, God, get me out of this situation. But may we be like Nehemiah—those who would pray for strength to continue the work and be steadfast in our responsibilities. When we pray for strength, God will deliver.

> I will praise you, O Lord, among the nations;
> I will sing of you among the peoples.
> For great is your love, reaching to the heavens;
>   your faithfulness reaches to the skies.
>   **(Psalm 57:9-10)**

Close out today by reading John 21:20-25. (If you are feeling ambitious, begin at v. 15.) **In your own words, what does John 21:22 say to you?**

_____

_____

_____

Peter, curious about John's destiny, asks, "Lord, what about him?" Christ replies, "What is that to you? You must follow Me."

In other words, "Don't look at others. Keep your eyes firmly fixed on Me!"

These are the same words Jesus wants us to hear from Him, "Don't be distracted by others and their call. Follow Me!" God has a plan and a destiny just for you. Be still in His presence and you will hear Him. Continue to follow Him.

Reflective prayer:
Write your thoughts, convictions, or insights.

_____

_____

_____

_____

_____

_____

_____

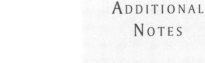

Day Three
An Encouraging Word

Continue studying Colossians 4:16-17 (NLT).

After you have read this letter, pass it on to the church at Laodicea so they can read it, too. And you should read the letter I wrote to them. And say to Archippus, "Be sure to carry out the ministry the Lord gave you."

Who was singled out for special encouragement in Colossians 4:17?

_____

Do you remember Archippus from Day One this week? While researching house churches, it is clear that the church met in the home of Philemon and Apphia, so Archippus was most likely their son. Just from this one little verse, we may wonder why Paul singled out Archippus. Could it have been that Archippus needed a little extra encouragement to continue the fierce battle against the false teachers? Paul must have realized that any ministry begun in the Lord should be seen through to completion.

WE MUST
CONTINUE
TO RUN
WITH
PURPOSE
IN EVERY
STEP.

GO DEEPER

 Look up the following Scriptures and identify the words of encouragement you find "to keep keeping on."

1 Corinthians 9:24-26

_____

_____

_____

Philippians 3:12-14

_____

_____

_____

2 Timothy 4:5

_____

_____

_____

Ladies, we already established back in the beginning of this study that the Christian walk takes hard work, discipline, and preparation. As Christians, we are running toward our heavenly reward. While we aspire for that day, we must continue to run with purpose in every step. Don't give up! Complete the work God has given you to do.

Are you in need of a little extra encouragement, like Archippus was? I asked my friends to pray for me as I finished writing *The Secret is Out*, "that I would end this study with as much passion as I began."

Is there something you need to finish well? Share with your group, so they can pray for you.

_____

_____

_____

Is there someone you need to encourage today? That person may be waiting for you to notice the work they are doing, and your words may be just what he or she needs to finish well.

_____

_____

_____

What does the end of Colossians 4:17 encourage Archippus to do?

_____

As you think about carrying out the work the Lord has given you and ending well, let's take a look at Matthew 25:14-30 and learn all we can from the three servants. Read the passage and then answer the following questions:

How did the man divide the talents among the servants (v. 15)?

_____

Record what each servant did with his talent.

The one with 5 talents _____

The one with 2 talents _____

The one with 1 talent _____

Write the respective responses of the master who returned from his trip.

The one with 5 talents _____

_____

The one with 2 talents _____

_____

The one with 1 talent _____

_____

What is the promise from Matthew 25:29?

_____

_____

_____

Oh ladies, that we would be women who diligently prepare for Christ's return by investing our talents and time to serve God! God will reward our faithfulness. Then, we will hear the words from Matthew 25:23: "Well done, good and faithful servant! You have been faithful with a few things; I will put you in charge of many things. Come and share your master's happiness!"

Close out today by reading 1 Timothy 4:15-16 (MSG).

> Cultivate these things. Immerse yourself in them. The people will all see you mature right before their eyes! Keep a firm grasp on both your character and your teaching. Don't be diverted. Just keep at it. Both you and those who hear you will experience salvation.

Reflective prayer:

Write your thoughts, convictions, or insights.

_____

_____

_____

_____

_____

_____

_____

_____

Day Four
Closing Words

Here we are, studying the last verse of the Book of Colossians. Begin by reading Colossians 4:18 and 2 Thessalonians 3:17. **How can you be sure this book was authored by Paul?**

_____

_____

_____

Most likely, Paul used a secretary who listened to his dictation and wrote the letter, with Paul writing the final greeting in his own handwriting to validate that the letter was genuine. This personal signature guarded against forged letters that some may have claimed came from Paul.

In the New Testament, thirteen epistles have been attributed to Paul. The lives Paul touched were changed and challenged by meeting Christ through him. Some say that no person, apart from Jesus Himself, shaped the history of Christianity like the apostle Paul.

What did Paul ask the Colossians to remember, according to verse 18 of chapter 4?

_____

In the Greek, "remember" *(mnemoneuo)*[1] means "to be mindful; recollect." I don't believe Paul was telling them to remember his chains so they would feel sorry for him, but to pray for him as he came to their minds.

It is the same thing as when you receive a newsletter from a missionary you support. You hear about their successes and struggles. Why? So you can be mindful of them and pray for them in a constructive way, especially since they are out there on the front lines.

Take a moment and think about those people you know who are struggling because they are proclaiming the Good News of Jesus Christ. Please pray for them. Maybe God is convicting you to send them an e-mail, write a note, or call them so that you can encourage them in their work for Christ. (I think I am going to listen to the teacher, stop what I'm doing, and practice what I teach by making a quick call. I'll be right back. Okay, I'm back.) Oh, that we could show our remembrance of these ministers by encouraging them today through our words and prayers.

As hard as Paul may have had it while he was confined to a prison and enchained, he always cared for those he was writing to and didn't focus all that much on his own concerns. I wonder what we would feel and say if we found ourselves in a similar position. Probably it would be something like this: "Remember my chains. Ask God to give me grace to get through what I need to as I face this trial." But listen to Paul's words: "Remember my chains. Grace be with you." It was not, "Grace be with me." One of the greatest evidences of spiritual maturity is the desire to reach out to others as you go through your own struggles.

GO DEEPER

 Read Luke 23:26-43 and John 19:25-27 about Jesus' ultimate love for others.

What concerned Jesus as He faced death?

_____

_____

_____

As you look at Paul and Jesus, how could you be more aware of others throughout your day?

_____

_____

_____

Okay, you may not be imprisoned physically, but you may feel imprisoned spiritually. You may feel trapped by a past sin, thought, or action. There is hope through Jesus Christ! Let's look into God's Word for encouragement through our spiritual struggles.

Read John 10:10, Romans 7:25, and 8:35-37 and answer the following questions:

 What does Jesus want to give us (John 10:10)?

_____

_____

ADDITIONAL
NOTES

Who is the answer for our lives (Romans 7:25)?

_____

_____

Who do we have victory through (Romans 8:35-37)?

_____

_____

Write any added insight you discovered from the previous verses.

_____

_____

_____

_____

_____

_____

Ladies, nothing can separate us from Christ's presence.

For I am convinced that neither death nor life, neither angels
nor demons, neither the present nor the future, nor any
powers, neither height nor depth, nor anything else in all
creation, will be able to separate us from the love of God
that is in Christ Jesus our Lord.

(Romans 8:38-39)

Reflective prayer:

Write your thoughts, convictions, or insights.

_____

_____

_____

_____

_____

_____

_____

_____

ADDITIONAL
NOTES

[1] Strong, The New Strong's Exhaustive Concordance of the Bible.

Day Five
Grace be unto You

Icannot begin to express to you what studying this wonderful book together has meant to me. It is bittersweet as I prepare for the last day of this Bible study. This has been an incredible time of deep study into the Word of God. Deuteronomy 29:29 says, "The secret things belong to the Lord our God, but the things revealed belong to us and to our children forever, that we may follow all the words of this law." These words ring deep in my heart as I ponder on all that we have learned from this amazing book. I pray that you will hold fast to all the truths God has revealed to you and walk in a manner worthy of His calling.

What closing blessings does Paul leave with his readers in Colossians 4:18, as with every other letter he wrote? For additional insight, look up 1 Corinthians 16:23, Galatians 6:18, and Ephesians 6:24.

_____

_____

Paul began this letter the same way he ended it: "May the grace of God be with you." Grace is the heart of Paul's message.

A reminder of the meaning of grace from Week One: "the free and unmerited favor of God, as manifested in the salvation of sinners (mankind) and the bestowal of blessings; God's riches at Christ's expense."

Look up the following Scriptures under their designated captions so that you can fully grasp and understand what God is trying to reveal to you through these profound verses. Discover how He is showing you the ways He can impart His divine power through you to enable you to live a victorious and overcoming life in Him.

Ladies, the power of the gospel is by grace.

 1. **We are saved by "grace" alone, through faith in Jesus Christ.**

Read Ephesians 2:4-8 and write what this Scripture means to you.

_____

_____

_____

_____

_____

_____

2. The power for Christian living comes by grace.

   Read 2 Corinthians 9:8 and Hebrews 4:14-16. Write what these Scriptures mean to you.

   _____

   _____

   _____

   _____

   _____

3. Every believer is dependent upon grace.

   Read Acts 13:43 and write what the Scripture means to you.

   _____

   _____

   _____

   _____

   _____

I hope this helps you to understand the grace of God a little better.

Dear sister, we need the power of God flowing and operating through us if we are going to achieve any real success in the Lord with whatever He is calling us to in this life. Without God's divine power and ability working through us, we will never reach the destination He is calling us to. We will never be able to reach the finish lines that God has in store for us unless we have the power of His Holy Spirit working in and through us.

As we live out this life in Christ, we must be encouraged to press on and find satisfaction in Him alone, for He is the giver of life and our strength for the here and now. Press on, dear sister; there is a reward for you far greater than you could ever imagine or hope for.

Read the following Scriptures and write what they mean to you personally as you continue in your faith and draw on the power of Jesus Christ in your everyday life.

Philippians 4:10-14

_____

_____

_____

_____

Psalm 16:11, 28:7, 90:14

_____

_____

_____

_____

PRESS ON,
DEAR SISTER.
THERE IS
A REWARD
FOR YOU
FAR GREATER
THAN YOU
COULD EVER
IMAGINE OR
HOPE FOR!

Ladies, life is not perfect when you follow Jesus wholeheartedly. It is pretty much guaranteed you will have trouble before entering the kingdom of God (Acts 14:22). But the good news is that He has overcome the world, so take heart and fight the good fight by praying continually. There is nothing better than conceding to the power of Christ in you!

The Book of Colossians put things and people in their proper places, while combating the false teachers of the day as they attempted to remove Jesus Christ from His proper place of absolute supremacy.

 Write the proper place each person/area should occupy, according to what we have studied from Colossians.

Jesus Christ (1:15, 17, 27)

_____

The Word (1:5-6, 3:16)

_____

Prayer (1:9-14, 4:2)

_____

Ambition (3:2, 23)

_____

Sandwiched in between are our responsibilities: to know the truth to help us avoid error, develop our character to be more Christ-like, and deepen our relationships with our church, family, and fellow laborers.

ADDITIONAL
NOTES

Please don't miss this exercise; it will be well worth your time.

Finish the day by taking a few minutes to skim the four chapters of Colossians one last time to see all that you have gleaned from our study.

What impacted you most from your study of Colossians?

_____

_____

_____

_____

What changes has this study made in your life?

_____

_____

_____

_____

MY HOPE IS:

YOU'VE
LEARNED IT.

YOU'RE
LIVING IT.

YOU'RE
PASSING IT ON.

My dear sister, I thank you for journeying along this road with me. I pray that you make your gifts available to the Savior. He will do extraordinary things with ordinary people who faithfully serve Him. Devote yourself to prayer about what God calls you to and how He wants you to faithfully serve Him.

Go be a blessing to someone!

Reflective prayer:

Write your thoughts, convictions, or insights.

ADDITIONAL
NOTES

_____

_____

_____

_____

_____

_____

_____

_____

_____

_____

Week Five
Video Session

Christ in Your Heart

Are you wondering what "born again" means and how you can ask Jesus into your heart? When I was searching and someone mentioned "born again" to me, my first thought was, "What is this? This seems a little radical to me." Then they explained, and I understood.

In the Book of John, Jesus has a conversation with a man named Nicodemus who approached Him, curious about the Kingdom of God.

Jesus told Nicodemus, "I tell you the truth, unless you are born again, you cannot see the Kingdom of God" (John 3:3 NLT). In the next verse Nicodemus responded, "How can an old man go back into his mother's womb and be born again?"

As a respected leader in the Jewish community, Nicodemus was a moral man who obeyed God's law. Even though he was a fine man, however, something was missing. Is something missing in your life? Does your heart feel like there is a hole in it?

Today, just like in the days of Nicodemus, many people confuse "being good" with a "born again" experience. New birth begins when the Holy Spirit convicts a person of sin. Because of the fall of man, we are spiritually dead and need a Savior. God so loved us that He provided a spiritual rebirth. All we have to do is ask Him for it. God's Word tells us that we are all sinners (Romans 3:23). Jesus died on a cross and was raised from the dead to save sinners (Colossians 1:20), and if we believe on the Lord Jesus, Scripture assures us we will be saved (Acts 16:31). Colossians 1:22 tells us that He has reconciled us by Christ's physical body through death to present us holy in his sight, without blemish and free from accusation. When we accept Jesus into our hearts and become born anew, we admit that we are sinful and tell God that we want to turn from our sinful ways (Acts 3:19). In this act of faith, we are rescued from the domain of darkness and transfered into the Kingdom of Light, Jesus Christ, in whom we have redemption, the forgiveness of sins (Colossians 1:13-14).

Jesus told Nicodemus that every person who believes in Christ would not perish but have eternal life (John 3:16). He is the way, the truth and the life; no one can come to the father but through Jesus Christ (John 14:6). To believe in Jesus is to be "born again."

Take this moment to confess your sins and ask Jesus to save you, and the Holy Spirit will come right away to live in your heart. Please don't put this important decision off. "For anyone who calls on the name of the Lord will be saved" (Acts 2:21).

Upon receiving Jesus Christ into your heart, share this important decision with another person—maybe your leader, spouse, or a dear friend. I pray that you will find a Bible-believing church to attend so you can continue to worship God, grow in Christ, and serve in the Spirit.

Dear sister, this is a day to rejoice and be happy. Congratulations on being "born again"!

Order Info.

For autographed copies, to order the DVD,
or to schedule speaking engagements, contact

Jessie Seneca
jessie@jessieseneca.com
610.216.2730

To order *The Secret is Out*, visit
www.MoreofHimMinistries.org

Also available from your favorite bookstore

Like us on Facebook

For bulk order discounts contact
Fruitbearer Publilshing, LLC
302.856.6649 • FAX 302.856.7742
info@fruitbearer.com
www.fruitbearer.com
P.O. Box 777, Georgetown, DE 19947